THE Telegraph BOOK OF THE
ASHES 2013

THE Telegraph BOOK OF THE

ASHES 2013

**Edited by
Stephen James**

First published in Great Britain
2013 by Aurum Press Ltd
74–77 White Lion Street
Islington
London N1 9PF
www.aurumpress.co.uk

A catalogue record for this book is
available from the British Library.

ISBN 978 1 78131 177 6

1 3 5 7 9 10 8 6 4 2
2013 2015 2017 2016 2014

Typeset in Sabon by SX Composing DTP, Rayleigh, Essex
Printed and bound by CPI Group (UK) Ltd, Croydon, CR0 4YY

Contents

Introduction

It used to be England that approached Ashes series in disarray, with selection seemingly involving the use of a hat from which names were picked at random.

But then Australia arrived in England in 2013. They had just lost a Test series 4-0 in India, during which four of their players – Shane Watson, Mitchell Johnson, James Pattinson and Usman Khawaja – had been suspended from the third Test for not completing an assignment given to them by coach Mickey Arthur. Unsurprisingly they became known as 'the homework four'.

Then there was the announcement of the Ashes party. That was equally shambolic. No one was sure when or where it was going to be unveiled. Its number? No one was sure of that either. As it was, 16 names were announced, including recalls for two 35-year-olds in Chris Rogers, who had played just one Test five years previously, and wicketkeeper Brad Haddin, who took over as vice-captain after a clearly piqued Watson had relinquished that role. But by the time of the first Test, two players not in that party – Steve Smith and 19-year-old debutant Ashton Agar – were selected to play at Trent Bridge.

That was because much had changed. First there was a remarkable incident in a Birmingham bar after Australia had lost to England by 48 runs in their first match of the ICC

Champions Trophy. There the Australian batsman David Warner punched England's Joe Root.

When it eventually came to light Warner was fined £7,000 and, although he remained with the Ashes squad, banned from all cricket until the first Test. And this came just three weeks after Warner had been fined £3,700 for a foul-mouthed rant against journalists on Twitter.

As it was, Warner was not selected for the first Test and was sent instead on the Australia A tour of Zimbabwe and South Africa. But there had obviously been a breakdown in culture and disciplinary ethos in the Australian squad long before.

Coach Arthur had been seen by many as a dead man walking ever since his suspension of 'the homework four', and so it proved: after Australia had finished bottom of their Champions Trophy group, Arthur was sensationally sacked, to be replaced by Darren Lehmann, already in England as coach of Australia A, with captain Michael Clarke also resigning as a selector. There were just 16 days to go before the start of the Ashes. You could not have made it up.

Unless, of course, it had happened during those grim years between 1989 and 2005 when Australia won all eight Ashes series at a canter.

But 2005 was when the tide had begun to turn, with England winning that home series in thrilling fashion. Yes, there was a haunting return to former thumpings with a 5-0 defeat for England Down Under in 2006/07, but the great Australian side was breaking up.

By the time of the 2009 series in England, Shane Warne,

Glenn McGrath, Matthew Hayden, Justin Langer, Adam Gilchrist, Damien Martyn and Jason Gillespie had all gone.

England won that series, just, but then inflicted a huge hiding upon Australia in their own back yard in 2010/11, winning three Tests by an innings to take the series 3-1.

Between that and the 2013 series Ricky Ponting and Mike Hussey had departed too. It looked as if Clarke would almost be fighting a lone battle in the batting stakes. England might have lost retired skipper Andrew Strauss' 21 Test centuries, but in their side for the first Test the batsmen could muster 82 Test centuries, Australia had 32, and 23 of those were Clarke's. And Clarke had been struggling with a back injury, meaning that George Bailey, a player not in the Ashes squad, had to lead the side in the Champions Trophy.

England's problems were piffling by comparison. They had experienced a dip after becoming the No 1-ranked Test side in 2011, losing that status to South Africa in 2012, but they had still beaten India away from home for the first time in 27 years later that year.

A drawn series in New Zealand (0-0) was disappointing, but the same opponents were immediately dispatched 2-0 with ease at home.

England's greatest selectorial headache centred around an opening partner for captain Alastair Cook. Somerset's Nick Compton had made two hundreds in New Zealand, but had conspicuously struggled at home. He was dropped. So, with Kevin Pietersen returning from a knee injury, the young Joe Root was promoted up the order.

But for all Australia's travails, the suspicion was that they had bottomed out. Lehmann was a sage choice; a pupil from the old school, but one of high cricketing intelligence and sound basic behavioural principles. His immediate selections, like re-promoting Watson to the top of the order, were shrewd.

Wednesday July 10, the date of the first Test, arrived quickly on the heels of a British and Irish Lions rugby series victory over Australia in Sydney on the previous Saturday and Andy Murray's Wimbledon triumph the following day.

England had not won three successive Ashes series since those of 1977, 1978/79 and 1981.

Expectations were high.

First Test Trent Bridge Day One

July 11 Derek Pringle

England (215) v Australia (75-4)

Ashes contests have struggled to live up to the sheer ding-dong nature of the 2005 series but Wednesday's play at Trent Bridge did a more than passable impression, with 14 wickets falling and a bowler on each side having the opportunity of a hat-trick.

It was the most wickets to fall on an opening day since the 17 at Lord's in 2005. On that occasion, England dismissed Australia but then collapsed to the unerring menace of Glenn McGrath, a setback they did not recover from during the match but did in the series, going on to win 2-1.

If seam and adrenalin caused the carnage at Lord's, it was swing and nerves that were the prime disposers of batsmen here, though the odd bad choice of shot and the application of poor technique were their close allies.

Under slate grey skies that lasted all day, and with Peter Siddle rampant in taking five for 50, England were dismissed for 215, to the great delight of the very vocal Australian contingent in the crowd.

Not that any crowing lasted long, despite Shane Watson's mini-assault on Steven Finn. With Watson trying to belt one drive too many to give Finn the first of two wickets in two balls, Australia lost four wickets, including their captain Michael Clarke for a duck, to finish an enthralling opening day still 140 runs behind England.

Clarke is a prize almost beyond rubies and it needed one of the better balls of James Anderson's career to get him. He later added Chris Rogers, though the left-hander can count himself unlucky that Hawk-Eye's track had the ball clipping leg stump rather than missing as the naked eye suggested.

With Australia's captain back in the hutch, Alastair Cook's team are just shading the honours but that could change quickly should any swing evaporate along with the grey cloud that enabled it on Wednesday, and should Stuart Broad remain an onlooker as he did during the final session.

Broad was struck a painful blow on his right shoulder by James Pattinson during his innings of 24, the one he had a cortisone jab in the week before. The overnight brief from England was that he had stayed off the field to have the joint iced as a precaution but he is still likely to be compromised by it should he resume duties.

The portents that this might be an unusual day's cricket began when Australia tore up the conventions of Test cricket by picking teenager Ashton Agar, a development spinner not even in the original Test squad.

If that was a left-arm selection from left field, the decision to send David Warner – widely tipped to play here – to Zimbabwe to get some match cricket with Australia A, was right only in the respect that the denizens of Harare's bars tend to hit back.

Many will have questioned Cook's decision to bat first after winning the toss, given the blanket cloud cover, especially after the way Australia's bowlers swung the ball. But swing is never guaranteed, as this year's crop of Nottinghamshire pace bowlers will tell you, and with the dry bare pitch the prime motivation behind Cook's decision-making, it was the right choice.

Having chosen to bat Cook at least owed his team a defiant innings once the ball began to hoop about. His new opening partner Joe Root looked calm enough and with his soft hands on the bat, was able to smother the swing.

Cook has more hard angles to his batting than Root and once his bat was drawn away from his body by Pattinson, an edge was more likely than not and likely to carry.

It was how Australia's pace bowler had got him out in the whitewash series of 2006-07, although he worked hard to cure himself by being scrupulous over which balls he played at wide of off stump. Whether from pressure or distraction, old foibles escape their leash from time to time and England's captain was not immune on Wednesday.

The wicket was against the run of play after Australia's bowlers made a nervy start. It was not until Root and Jonathan Trott had added 51 for the second wicket that Siddle got into his stride having leaked 27 runs off his first four overs.

Firing the ball full at Root's middle stump he got some late outswing to defeat the hasty rearrangement of his footwork. Shane Warne had said Australia would bowl full at him to get him out and this one was right on the money.

Kevin Pietersen followed, edging one that Siddle shaped away from him. He had already been dropped, on one, when Brad Haddin failed to intercept a leg glance off Pattinson, but that did not appear to affect him as he reeled off a couple of sumptuous boundaries. But before Haddin could rue his miss, his hard push off Siddle had been snaffled by Clarke at second slip.

The swinging ball had not tethered England's batsmen as boundaries flowed. In fact, boundaries comprised 70.69 per cent of their total, the highest they had managed in the first innings of a Test since 1961 at Old Trafford, also an Ashes Test.

For once, Jonathan Trott was the greatest contributor of fours, his role as England's rock shelved while he put away the sundry bad balls sent down by Australia's pacemen. Trent Bridge has not been a good ground for him or Cook. The pair have played 19 innings between them here and never reached fifty, a milestone Trott fell two short of after he dragged on a wide one from Siddle.

Ian Bell edged a good outswinger from Siddle to Watson at first slip, that having been delivered wide on the crease drew him into playing it. In the lead-in to this match, Siddle had looked out of sorts. But the competitive nature that clearly stirs within, and which is released at the first whiff of Pommy blood, transformed him into an unlikely destroyer, a role he completed when Matt Prior wafted a wide ball to short cover to spring a trap a blind rhinoceros would have seen.

As he tired, Starc and Pattinson took up the cudgels. Jonny Bairstow had as little match cricket as Warner coming into this game but he overcame it to play a fine innings until his old habit of playing across and over a straight half-volley gave Starc his first wicket.

Starc then had another next ball, when Finn wafted away from his body and nicked to Haddin. His hat-trick ball was close but no cigar, but this was a day when any satisfaction on either side was short-lived.

July 11 Paul Hayward

This Ashes series is going to be nasty, brutish and short if it carries on like this. Not for us, the voyeurs, but certainly for the players, who tossed away 14 wickets without any batsman reaching 50.

An eagerness to do too much resulted in most of the 22 offering way too little on a day of rampant anxiety.

Five days after a Lions series win and three nights after Andy Murray's crushing of Novak Djokovic at Wimbledon the home crowd gathered beside the Trent wanting another fiesta. A marching band and Red Arrows fly-past set the domineering tone.

The motley crew assembled by Australia included a 19-year-old debutant spinner (Ashton Agar) and a 35-year-old short-sighted and colour-blind opener (Chris Rogers) who last wore the Baggy Green 62 Tests or 5½ years ago.

But the master-underdog narrative wrapped round this series soon disintegrated. The peculiar intensity of day one of an Ashes battle played havoc with the script. Calmer heads counselled against premature English triumphalism.

Yet who could ignore the evidence of a coach being

sacked two weeks before the series, a punch being thrown in Birmingham's Walkabout bar or the inexperience and downright statistical mediocrity of some of Australia's squad?

But what distinguishes the Ashes from other cricket marathons? The levelling force of history, the power of patriotism, the weight of individual defiance, as expressed by Peter Siddle, who even the Cricket Australia website describes as the 'workhorse' of this attack.

'There were a lot of eager blokes, first Test, first day of an Ashes series,' Siddle agreed after taking five for 50. Joe Root, Jonathan Trott, Kevin Pietersen, Ian Bell and Matt Prior all fell to the 'Victorian Vegan', as Siddle became known when he gave up meat (an unsustainable folly, according to fast-bowling carnivores of earlier vintages).

The first ball, so often treated as a flaming symbolic memo from the heavens, bounced high and wide from the fist of James Pattinson, who is intent in avenging the poor treatment of his brother, Darren – picked for one Test by England then dumped.

Not quite 'a Harmie', the label attached to all 11am spray-balls in honour of Steve Harmison, Pattinson's first effort was a neat illustration of what nerves can do to the protagonists.

If you like suicidal batting and short bursts of demonic bowling then this was the Test for you. The tap-tap of feet on pavilion steps went on all day from Alastair Cook's dismissal to the removal of Rogers to leave Australia 53 for four.

As a measure of the disorder, the two captains managed 13 runs between them – and all of those were Cook's. The leg-cutter from Jimmy Anderson that impaled Michael Clarke for nought was a comfortable winner of the Wednesday beauty contest.

The Ashes have probably never brought together two such angelic-faced captains, but their conflict will not repeat this pattern across five Tests stretching to The Oval in late August.

Cook was impetuous driving at Pattinson and gave Australia the scent of blood they needed. Pattinson and Mitchell Starc were wild at times but still flashed that edge of youthful menace their team will need in years to come.

Only five times since 1905 have 13 or more wickets fallen on the opening day of an Ashes series and too many of England's were surrendered lightly.

Modern sports stars pretend to know how to objectify hype – to block it out – but few can say they have really mastered the art. The more they say 'we have to treat it as just another Test match' the more the other side of the brain is gripped by panic.

'The occasion,' that wrecker of sleep and destroyer of equilibrium, still comes under the mind's door like fog.

Example: Shane Watson, the opener, wafts at James Anderson in the first over. After a few meaty blows he drives at a ball from Finn and is caught in the slips by Root.

Example: for Finn's very next delivery, Ed Cowan, who might like to think about hanging around a while to justify his selection, swipes at a bullet ball moving away from him and is caught by Graeme Swann.

This puts Finn on a hat-trick against Cowan's captain,

Clarke, who only just survives a snorter that flies past his off-stump.

So where were we? England, fragile with the bat, occasionally inspired with the ball.

Australia: promising with the ball, then reckless and/or exposed with the bat.

As the Trent Bridge scorers flopped down for a rest, Phil Hughes and Steve Smith were holding Australia's innings together at 75 for four, and plans were being hatched for other entertainment on Sunday at the latest.

Each player will have closed his hotel door glad this first day had passed. The successes will have slept inspired and the underachievers will know the scrutiny will be merciless.

Already we can say England are superior in individual talent, experience and team balance. Australia, under a new, old-school coach, must hope Starc and Pattinson add accuracy to their enthusiasm, that Siddle keeps knocking over English batsmen without seeming to do very much and that their top six batters are better and more sensible than they looked in the opening exchanges.

Hot clear weather would give both sides a chance to settle down and play themselves into this series. Day one offered no such comfort. It was all about victims and volatility.

July 11 Scyld Berry

It was a great day for Test cricket. It was not a great day of Test cricket.

It was a day when the vast majority of batsmen on both

sides misheard the umpire's call of 'Play!' and thought he had said 'Charge!'

Officers and men threw themselves into the fray without any thought for their own survival. Only a careful few looked over the parapet first: Joe Root and Jonathan Trott, Chris Rogers and Steve Smith, that was about it.

Emotion overwhelmed reason throughout a sultry day – which is not, of course, the first time it has happened on the opening day of an Ashes series.

England's most cautious batsman, Alastair Cook, who has spent his whole career in self-abnegation, set the tone by throwing his bat at a wide ball. Australia's most cautious batsman, Ed Cowan, wasted not a moment in following suit.

It was much the same at Lord's on the opening day of the 2005 series when 17 wickets fell. The standard then, however, was higher than yesterday as some wonderful bowlers were at work: England's four fine quick bowlers and, finer still, Glenn McGrath.

It was much the same, too, at Edgbaston in 1997 when 13 wickets fell on the opening day. That was the last time that England batted well on the first day of an Ashes series, for after tumbling out Australia for 118 they reached 200 for three by the close.

In both of these cases, and again yesterday, the collapses were attributable not only to the emotion of the occasion but to the type of cricket that the batsmen of both sides had been playing in the build-up.

When players spend the first half of the summer, or at least the preceding few weeks, playing one-day cricket, they are loath to leave a ball or play a defensive shot when the Tests begin.

The authorities who plan for opening ceremonies and fly-pasts also have a part in over-hyping players and scrambling their brains, after the build-up that comes with every Ashes series.

In addition to the emotion of the occasion, and the one-day cricket these sides have been playing since the start of the Champions Trophy, the technique of the modern batsman against swing leaves a lot for Geoffrey Boycott to desire.

Root demonstrated how the swinging ball should be played – under the nose, with soft hands – and had to be got out. The rest of the England order contributed to their downfall with 'batsman-error': drives in most cases, or a too-firm push in Kevin Pietersen's, or an open-faced steer in Ian Bell's.

Quick singles to rotate the strike and disrupt the bowler? Nothing so old-fashioned, thank you. Just fling the bat and see how many boundaries you can hit. Hence the astonishing statistic that England, out of their 194 runs off the bat, scored 152 in fours. No England batsman scored more than four singles.

England are not alone, of course. Pakistan were even more incapable against swing on this ground in 2010, dismissed by James Anderson for 80. New Zealand in their last Test here scored 123, India 158, and West Indies 165.

Big bats and little patience. There is no glamour attached, no Indian Premier League contract, to hanging in and surviving.

But it made for a fascinating and fluctuating day – one

that is great for the future of Test cricket – because it proved that, however prepared and programmed Test cricketers are, a few of them will rise to a great occasion and most will sink to it.

Cowan has an ingenious cricket brain, as he showed in his book about an Australian domestic season. He is capable of such self-analysis as this sentence: 'I played an absolutely horrendous shot trying to impose myself a disgracefully undisciplined cover-drive to a wide ball.'

And blow me down, mate, what does Cowan do when facing his first ball in a Test match in England, but play a disgracefully undisciplined cover-drive to a wide ball.

Australia's young opening bowlers were carried away too: the runs conceded by Mitchell Starc and James Pattinson before tightening up, and by Ashton Agar when he was curiously selected and given a bowl instead of Shane Watson, will likely prove decisive. But Peter Siddle bowled flawlessly once he switched to the Radcliffe Road and went from bowling like Bruce Lee to Brett Lee, taking five for 23.

Coaches will never be able to turn Test cricketers into robots – not batsmen at any rate. There is too much time for too many thoughts to flow through their heads and too much adrenalin through their veins. The 50-over and 20-over formats become ever more formulaic, but Test cricket will never be predictable so long as it is played by humans.

Day Two

July 12 Derek Pringle

England (215 & 80-2) lead Australia (280) by 15 runs

We live in an age of wonders but when a teenager plucked from relative obscurity scores 98 on his Ashes debut batting at No 11, as Ashton Agar did against England here on Thursday, our disbelief enters new realms.

Agar, 19, and with 10 first-class games before his Test debut, shocked the cricket world on Wednesday when Australia selected him as their spinner. But if that was not surprise enough, he announced himself afresh with a record in his maiden Test innings, his 98 becoming the highest score by a No 11 after it surpassed the 95 made by Tino Best against England last year at Edgbaston.

His innings was not without controversy, from Alastair Cook's timid captaincy during its construction, to the stumping England felt they had off Graeme Swann, but which Marais Erasmus, the TV umpire, failed to grant when Agar was on six.

It was a game-changing moment and Matt Prior was so convinced that he demanded a second look, from Sky, after England had eventually finished fielding. But with one camera angle suggesting Agar's foot was still lifted, and another making it appear grounded, you could perhaps understand, in the absence of categoric evidence, why Erasmus gave the left-hander the benefit of the doubt. Less clear is why Jonathan Trott was not reprieved by the same principle when Australia reviewed an lbw shout from Mitchell Starc, when visual evidence suggested the ball had taken a slither of inside edge.

The protocol for referred decisions is that there must be strong TV evidence to overturn the umpire's original decision, which in Trott's case was a not out from Aleem Dar. What Erasmus did, when Michael Clarke called for the review, was the opposite, ignoring the visual snippet that supported Dar's original call. He was probably hoping to rely on Hot Spot to provide the clinching detail, but that was not available as it was still processing Joe Root's dismissal, following his caught behind the previous ball.

If those setbacks caused widespread ire among England's supporters, only ardent jingoists could claim not to have been disappointed for Agar when he fell two runs short, after hooking Stuart Broad's bouncer to Graeme Swann at deep-midwicket. Steve Waugh once said there were no fairytales in sport, but this still felt like one.

His 163-run partnership for the last wicket with Phil Hughes, who made a fine unbeaten 81, smashed other records, including the highest last-wicket partnership, which previously stood at 151. It was also only the third time in Test history that the last wicket has more than doubled the team's score, Australia recovering from an ignominious 117 for nine to 280, a lead of 65.

In a low-scoring game that can be a decisive advantage, though with batting conditions having eased from the first four sessions, Cook and Kevin Pietersen managed to stop Australia's rampaging momentum to enable England to end the day on 80 for two.

Both men were made to battle hard as Australia's bowlers settled for discipline over the destruction that threatened when Starc found himself on the second hat-trick opportunity of the match after dismissing Root and Trott in successive balls.

The ball swung in on both occasions, though Root, who had survived a close lbw off Starc when he was on nought, was a tad unlucky to be caught down the leg side. Indeed, there were suggestions, from Hot Spot, that he would have been reprieved had he reviewed it, though following a brief discussion with Cook he chose not to. Unlike the first innings, Cook was far more judicious in choosing which balls he played. But if that is his forte, his captaincy after James Anderson had reduced Australia's innings to cinders, following a brilliant exposition of reverse-swing bowling, was timid given the strong position his team were in.

From Australia's relatively healthy 108 for four, a score that owed much to Steve Smith's pugnacious 53, Anderson took three wickets in 13 balls including Smith's. With Swann chipping in by snaring Brad Haddin and James Pattinson, Australia lost five wickets for nine runs in 31 balls.

Mark Taylor, one of Australia's best captains, reckoned successful Test teams recognised the big moments and won them. With Agar coming to the crease with two balls to face from Swann, Cook pushed his field deep and let him get off the mark second ball with a push into the covers.

The ploy was done so he would face Anderson the next over, but if that is a reasonable plan for most No 11s, it involved a clear misunderstanding of the psychology of debutants. Getting off the mark would have seen a tidal wave of relief wash over

Agar, who quickly revealed a solid defence and neat line in wristy scoring shots. But if England were expecting Agar jelly to dissolve with nerves they got Agar the Horrible instead, as both Finn and Swann were belted around Trent Bridge.

With Stuart Broad still ailing from his bruised shoulder, Cook's other error was to replace Anderson, his star bowler, with Finn, who has so far flattered to deceive. With Hughes in attendance but never leading, Agar produced the finest innings of the match so far.

Tailenders often get lucky but this was no hit and hope. If anything it was hit and expect as Swann was drilled for two sixes and Finn pulled and then driven for boundaries. For any Test innings over fifty to rattle along at a run-a-ball is exceptional, but for a 19-year old novice to do it on an occasion that claimed many victims to nerves was remarkable.

His highest score for Henley, the English club side he played for in May, was 65 against Aston Rowant, but he batted at four then. This knock was mind-bogglingly better than that one, though watching him take in the adoration as if it was the most natural thing in the world, you would not have known it.

There is still a lot of cricket to be played in this Test but, whatever the outcome, his mark on it is already indelible.

July 12 Nick Hoult

England received a double apology over the failure of the Hotspot system to work during the controversial dismissal of Jonathan Trott.

The ICC chief executive Dave Richardson apologised to Giles Clarke, the chairman of the ECB, for the fact the Hotspot camera was not able to determine whether or not Trott edged a delivery from Mitcehll Starc before it hit his front pad. Third umpire, Marais Erasmus, overturned the decision of on field official Aleem Dar to give Trott out lbw despite the act the side on Hotspot image of the dismissal was not available.

A furious Andy Flower demanded an explanation from match referee Ranjan Madugalle, the ICC's most senior official, over the lbw dismissal. England want to know why Trott was given out and if the the match officials followed the proper protocols.

Sky explained that the Hot Spot camera missed the Trott wicket as it was replaying Joe Root's dismissal a ball earlier. Images cannot be replayed and played at the same time.

'He was given not out on the field and it is frustrating it got overruled,' James Anderson said. 'He has hit the ball and he has been given not out. We are all for technology. Since it has come in, more decisions get given out correctly than wrongly. From our point of view we want it.'

The inventor of the Hotspot system also apologised blaming the malfunction on 'operator error'.

'Here is the absolute truth from our perspective in regard to the Trott incident,' said Warren Brennan.

'It was operator error. My operator did not trigger the system in order to cater for the Trott delivery. Instead the operator sat on the Root delivery in order to offer a replay from the previous ball and did not realise until it was too late that he should have triggered the system for the Trott delivery as the priority. Simple mistake, something that anyone could have made but my Hot Spot operator has worked on the system since 2007 and to my knowledge this is the first serious mistake he has made.'

Hot Spot is provided by an independent company for both Sky and the ICC. David Gower, the Sky commentator, said on air that the Hot Spot team were reviewing their protocols after the incident.

The Daily Telegraph also understands that Richardson has spoken to Clarke to explain the situation. Trott was convinced he hit the ball and a close-up slow-motion replay suggested it deviated as it went past the bat. The 'Snickometer', which is not part of the official review system, also detected a faint edge. The replay taken from square leg using Hot Spot thermal imaging could have proved whether Trott had struck the ball but Erasmus was able to view only shots picked up from behind the bowler's arm, which showed no mark on the bat.

Normally the third umpire overturns a decision only if there is conclusive evidence of an error, but Erasmus gave Trott out. An apparently bewildered Dar shook his head as he sent a stunned Trott on his way.

It was not the only controversial moment yesterday and Flower also queried the earlier decision to rule Australia's hero of the day, Ashton Agar, not out after England thought they had him stumped on six.

Matt Prior was convinced Agar was out and asked to view the Sky footage at the end of the Australia innings.

'I thought it was out. I saw it on the big screen, and it is hard to tell sometimes on that but Prior was pretty confident,' Anderson said.

Root should also have been given not out – Hot Spot showed he made no contact with the ball before it was caught down the leg side by Brad Haddin – but the England opener chose not to review the decision.

Flower has visited the match referee's room before after being angered by decisions. In South Africa four years ago he was enraged when third umpire Daryl Harper did not give Graeme Smith out caught behind amid accusations he failed to hear an edge because he did not turn up the volume on his monitor. The ICC launched an inquiry which concluded the sound feed was faulty.

Flower also asked for clarification from Javagal Srinath in Dubai in Jan 2012 when Andrew Strauss was given out caught behind.

July 12 Paul Hayward

The greatest innings by a No 11 batsman in Test cricket was also one of the finest in Ashes history, because it arrived from the bat of a 19-year-old with his team dangling at 117 for nine.

Add those extra elements of youth and pressure to a swashbuckling knock of 98 and Ashton Charles Agar was guaranteed a place in folklore 24 hours after taking delivery of his Baggy Green cap.

Seldom, if ever, have so many English observers wanted

an Australian to reach his century, or groaned when he fell short. The collective 'aah' that ran round Trent Bridge marked a brief cessation in hostilities, like Andrew Flintoff crouching to console Brett Lee at Edgbaston in 2005.

The two sides met in No-man's-land to acclaim an innings of great style as well as fortitude. All he must do now is live up to this promise.

'I was surprised by the support I was getting from the whole crowd,' Agar said. 'There was a little bit of sympathy from them too, which was nice to hear.'

Even Graeme Swann, who caught him at deep midwicket from a Stuart Broad delivery, ran over to commiserate. As the man who shot Bambi, Swann was at first exultant and then vaguely contrite. 'Well done, young fella,' said Swann as his victim left the field.

If the romance of Australia's record 10th-wicket partnership of 163 was lost on Alastair Cook's men, they could hardly fail to salute Agar's audacity in posting Australia's highest score with the bat after starting at 100-1 to achieve that feat.

To pass Tino Best's 11th-man Test record of 95 Agar had to survive a stumping appeal on six but surprisingly England's players resisted the urge to sledge the young upstart as he carried on with his innings.

'They didn't say a word to me,' Agar said, although, in England's second innings, Kevin Pietersen clearly fought an urge to smash him all the way to Nottingham Forest's ground.

We have seen the last of him at No 11. The rabbit's role is

not for people who can crash 98 runs all around the ground. Darren Lehmann, the coach, must have known the young hip-hop fan was too good to be last man in. But if the intention was to protect him from another day of scrutiny then Lehmann landed an unexpected bonus.

With Steve Smith scoring 53, both the new coach's late wild card picks from the Australia A tour paid off.

On his first, wicketless day here, all the talk was of Agar's bowling and how he had ousted Nathan Lyon from the spinner's job. Nobody thought to ask how he might get on with a bat. But then in he came to join another lefty, Phil Hughes, with Australia's batting open to ridicule, and by the time he departed the visitors were 65 ahead and all beaming on the balcony.

'I was put into the side to take wickets and I'm still very, very hungry to do that,' Agar said after bowling nine overs for 29 runs. 'I consider myself a bowling all-rounder. To get a wicket would be an extra special moment.'

Agar looks a bit like Australia's leading golfer, Adam Scott, and plays with something of the Masters champion's panache. His 12 fours and two sixes off 101 balls would have earned high rank in the annals of great defiant innings in any match in any circumstances. In this one he saved his country.

'Darren Lehmann told me to go and bat in my natural style and that's the way I like to play. I've batted at No 11 before in Queensland and was fortunate enough to get 50. I was lucky enough to have a good partner at the other end in Phil Hughes, who's a seriously, seriously good player.

He really, really helped me through it. He said to just keep watching the ball hard and playing ball by ball.

'I last made a hundred at Grade level for the University of Western Australia,' he added. He also scored a half century for Henley, who play in the Home Counties Premier League. Before that, Australia's 434th Test cricketer was playing Second XI cricket in Melbourne for Richmond before moving to Western Australia, where he made his first-class debut earlier this year. No wonder his brother William called his innings here 'surreal'.

A law student who suspended his studies to concentrate on a blossoming cricket career, the ultimate Ashes bolter also broke Glenn McGrath's Australian record of 61 by a No 11, striking 35 per cent of Australia's first innings runs. According to ESPNcricinfo, the all-time average for No 11 batsmen was 8.56.

So was this a life-changing day? 'Yeah it could be,' he said. 'It's a dream come true, that's what it is for me.'

At the end Clarke's men backslapped him up the pavilion steps and into a gilded future. Later he stood in the evening sun as Australian fans called his name and gathered around him for pictures. The glow from his face expressed his innocence as well as his pride.

'A lot of people are saying it's tragic you didn't make a hundred but it was brilliant that you made 98. How do you see it?' an Australian reporter asked. Agar said: 'Exactly the way you see it. I'm super-happy.'

July 12 Simon Hughes

Through history, most Test captains have been batsmen.

Originally, captaincy was the exclusive domain of amateurs, and the majority of amateurs were batsmen. The trend has continued, since bowlers anyway are generally typecast as brainless and/or too immersed in the strenuous business of bowling to be able to make rational team-orientated judgments in the heat of battle.

There is some sense in this. The one time it falls down is during extensive last-wicket partnerships when the fielding captain is an opening batsman. When the last-wicket pair are in, the opposing openers are thinking predominantly about batting, preparing themselves mentally for their innings, which could be only 10 minutes away. That was understandably the case with Alastair Cook for the first part of Australia's extraordinary 10th-wicket stand.

Having seen Australia suddenly lose five wickets for nine runs, Cook assumed the same pair of bowlers – James Anderson and Graeme Swann – would polish the innings off. Cook would not have known that Ashton Agar had more of a reputation as a batsman than a bowler and that he has 'play with no fear' written on his bedroom wall.

Anderson, who had bowled exceptionally for 80 minutes, was rested after two more overs and replaced by Steven Finn. Rhythm has proved elusive to Finn recently, however, and there was no intensity to his bowling. Agar found his shorter ball appetising. He helped himself to three boundaries through the square-leg region and, when Finn pitched up, he was flashed through extra cover with aplomb.

Swann, who had a stumping appeal rejected by the third umpire that on another day might have gone his way, was deftly swept for four, scythed through extra cover and majestically driven into the stand over long-off. In the commentary box, Geoffrey Boycott uttered the words 'Garfield Sobers', reminding us that the great West Indian began life at No 8 in the batting order. Almost in the blink of an eye, Agar was 43 not out.

Cook, realising he had to be proactive, but trying to protect Stuart Broad from aggravating his shoulder injury, brought back Anderson. He had only had half-an-hour's rest and Agar twice clubbed him through midwicket and brought up his fifty with a neat glide.

To celebrate, he sashayed down the wicket and launched Swann into the pavilion. Broad was introduced but, with an old ball, found the pitch unresponsive and the batsmen unbudgeable. It was only when Agar had impudently thumped the overworked Anderson back past him and he was into the 80s that England really changed tack.

Broad set three men back on the legside and aimed a succession of deliveries into his ribs, which required some considerable effort as the left-hander is 6ft 3in.

After handling it capably, and smartly, too, riding the bounce and dropping the ball into gaps, he finally perished, striking his pull so cleanly it carried all the way to deep midwicket to deny him a century that all but the most xenophobic would say he deserved.

Could England have done more? They might certainly have reverted to the bouncer tactic earlier. Perhaps the ease with which Agar dispatched the short balls bowled by Finn was a deterrent.

There was also no attempt from the faster bowlers to try a slower ball, always a useful tool against a player with a big backlift looking to strike the ball on the up.

But, on an essentially benign pitch with an old ball against a previously unseen player who showed remarkable aptitude and composure, it may not have made much difference.

This was an innings of quite breathtaking range and ambition from a teenager who looked as technically proficient as any of the old lags in the Australian side. It was a masterstroke, hiding their best player at No 11. Cook's best hope is that Agar goes up the order and has to face fresher bowlers with a harder ball.

Day Three
July 13 Derek Pringle

England (326-6 and 215) lead Australia (280) by 261 runs

After the hurly-burly of the first two days this Test was settling down into something approaching traditional Test cricket when Stuart Broad did that most Australian of things, he edged a catch and did not walk.

At that point Australia's indignation reached a pitch not seen since Ricky Ponting was run out here eight years again by 12th man Gary Pratt, and the match gained the animosity absent during the cut and thrust of the opening act.

Ponting's run out, which had the added theatre of a tirade against Duncan Fletcher, England's coach, was widely regarded as one of the major turning points of that series.

This moment was less crucial with England in a strong, though not entirely unassailable, position. Ian Bell was on 77 and the lead was 232.

A quick mop up of the tail by Australia's bowlers though would have made for a good contest today, an ambition that had receded by the close when Bell and Broad had extended their partnership to 108 and their team's lead to 261.

Most international cricketers do not walk, as Michael Clarke and his team are aware, though few perhaps try it on when the edge is as obvious as Broad's was on Friday.

Predictably, after the loud complaints made by England's camp the previous day, about Jonathan Trott's lbw (which came off an inside edge) and Matt Prior's stumping of Ashton Agar when he was on six, Australia saw the futility in escalating the hostility and played the incident down.

Agar was bowling his left-arm spin into the rough outside off-stump when Broad stepped back to cut, the ball taking an edge thick enough to strike Brad Haddin on the thigh before rebounding to Michael Clarke at slip.

It was so obvious that Sky's graphics man had already changed the scoreboard to read 297-7, though that was quickly rejigged when Aleem Dar's finger stayed down.

Regular onlookers wonder how Aleem Dar, one of the most highly respected of umpires on the International Cricket Council's elite panel, could have missed such an obvious deflection.

But he may have been fooled into thinking, not least by Broad's brazen poker face, that the main deflection had come not off the bat but Haddin's thigh.

To make matters worse, Broad was later given an official warning by the umpires for running on the pitch, a double dose of gamesmanship from England's fast bowler on his home ground.

Australia's disbelief was obvious from the way they appealed twice, once as formality at the obviousness of it all, the second time in that panicked way that suggested Franz Kafka had suddenly taken up umpiring and that it was all some grand conspiracy against them.

The matter would have been easily settled, in theory, had they been able to review the decision but Clarke had used up his team's second and final review on an optimistic lbw shout from Shane Watson against Bell.

The ball, swinging down leg, would not have hit another set of stumps but Clarke, perhaps wanting to appease a man with whom he has not been on best terms with, asked for it to be referred.

Following England's experience the previous day, the England and Wales Cricket Board have let it be known that they, and Australia, want unlimited reviews.

If technology is to be used, they argue, it must not be limited, though both boards recognise that the technology and the umpire protocols for using it need to become more robust.

India, as has been their stance for a while, are against the use of technology, the current confusion strengthening their case.

The incident certainly distracted them. Bell was dropped by Haddin off Peter Siddle in the next over, and James Pattinson was given a ticking off by umpire Kumar Dharmasena for general chuntering after Bell survived an optimistic lbw appeal from him that took a big inside edge.

Bell, in one of the more significant innings of his career, had batted the situation. Rather than disappear into that little world of his where style trumps substance, he settled not for how but how many.

The last time he had such a positive influence in the game, assuming the next two days throws up a positive result for England, was in the 2009 Durban Test against South Africa.

England won that game and should do so again here, but they will require Graeme Swann to be close to his best as well as make the new ball count.

Bell took control after Alastair Cook and Kevin Pietersen had added 110 runs for the third wicket to settle any immediate nerves after they resumed the day on 80-2, just 15 runs ahead.

His classic technique kept him safe on a pitch that has slowed but on which variable bounce off the cracks and turn out of the bowlers' footholes still offered occasional peril.

During his innings, which contained many of his signature shots, the molasses smooth cover drives and the filigree late cuts, he passed 6,000 Test runs.

He certainly looked more at ease with the pitch than anyone bar Pietersen, though the sluggish nature of the surface forced him to wear his sensible hat.

Both he and Cook were out playing across the ball, always

a risk when the ball is not coming on to the bat as it should. Agar got the England captain, a prize maiden Test wicket to go with his unforgettable innings on Thursday.

He later got Jonny Bairstow with one that turned off the main part of the pitch, but it was the edge he forced off Broad that would have given his team hope, now largely dashed, should England bowlers get it anywhere near right on day four.

July 13 Paul Hayward

Modern sport is peppered with examples of players declining to turn themselves into the authorities. Moral self-policing is rare.

If there was ever a true Spirit of Cricket, it took the day off at Trent Bridge when Stuart Broad blatantly nicked a delivery to first slip but chose not to walk.

Social media erupted with an amazing array of verdicts, ranging from cheat to sensible, from skulduggery to under-standable opportunism.

Not for the first time the argument veered off in the direction of moral equivalence. Would an Australian batsman say he would walk in those circumstances? If no, presumably, the problem goes away because we are all as cynical as each other. If yes, the Aussies are telling porkies. A vital moral question soon became another Ashes bunfight.

Temperatures were already running high here from the Jonathan Trott dismissal the day before. Not that personal rectitude was at stake when a not-out lbw call against Trott was overturned, despite Hot Spot being unavailable.

That decision by Marais Erasmus, the third umpire, cast doubt on the protocols for the use of technology. But it was an arcane procedural argument compared to the furore over Broad, which was witnessed by millions on television and unleashed a kind of Twitter hell.

Watching Broad stand his ground after Aleem Dar had failed to hear or see a thick edge off an Ashton Agar delivery was Darren Lehmann, the Australia coach, who played in the game made famous by Adam Gilchrist's walk, 10 years ago, in a semi-final against Sri Lanka of the Cricket World Cup.

Gilchrist is the starting point on walking, which is defined as 'the act of a batsman giving himself out, without waiting for an umpire's decision'. In his autobiography, which he even called Walking to Victory, Gilchrist recalled the moment an Aravinda de Silva ball popped off his bat and into the wicketkeeper's gloves.

'Then, to see the umpire shaking his head, meaning, "Not out", gave me the strangest feeling,' Gilchrist wrote. 'I don't recall what my exact thoughts were, but somewhere in the back of my mind, all that history from the Ashes series was swirling around.

'Michael Vaughan, Nasser Hussain and other batsmen, both in my team and against us, who had stood their ground in those "close" catching incidents were definitely a factor in what happened in the following seconds.

'I had spent all summer wondering if it was possible to take ownership of these incidents and still be successful. I had wondered what I would do. I was about to find out. The voice in my head was emphatic. Go. Walk. And I did.

'It was a really weird sensation to go against the grain of what 99 per cent of cricketers do these days, and what we've been doing for our whole careers. I was annoyed because I felt like I was batting well and had the chance to lay the foundation for a big team score – and it was me taking that away from myself.'

Some hailed Gilchrist as a groundbreaker. But everyone knows many in his team were livid, and turned on him, for a supposedly needless show of honesty. Ethics aside, the counter-case against Gilchrist's noble act was he had performed the umpire's job for him when his real obligation was to help Australia win the match.

He described his team-mates as 'flabbergasted' but said: 'I kept going back to the fact that, well, at the end of the day, I had been honest with myself. I felt it was time that players made a stand to take back responsibility for the game. I was at ease with that. The more I thought about it, the more settled I became with what I'd done.'

The heart soars to read this passage. But we know it does not correspond to the modern world of sport. Michael Clarke, the Australia captain, who took the Broad catch, has himself apologised for not walking in a match (he was dismissed on review).

Similarly it could be argued that Clarke frittered away his reviews and was thus unable to challenge Aleem Dar's inexplicable failure to see that Broad was out.

An absorbing moral ping-pong match ensued. What if it

had been the thinnest of edges instead of a thick one? Was it the obviousness of deflection that stained Broad's reputation? Should we expect one man to walk if he has seen countless others stand their ground?

An example that flew to mind, at another Nottinghamshire venue, was Liverpool's Luis Suárez handling the ball in an FA Cup tie against Mansfield and then walking it into the net.

At first, Suárez was excoriated as a villain. Then some came round to the view that it was the duty of the three match officials to see the offence, not the job of the player to own up to the offence.

Most ex-players at Trent Bridge tended to see it merely as a particularly flagrant example of an ingrained habit, ie not walking. Of course Aleem Dar should have seen it. Of course Australia should have had a review left to ensure Broad was brought to justice.

And of course Broad should have walked, in the strictly moral sense, rather than staying on to score 10 more runs and help strengthen England's hold on this first Test.

In the age of match and spot fixing, though, we already knew cricket is no Utopia.

July 13 Scyld Berry

It was Ian Bell's toughest, most valuable and best Test innings, whether or not he adds five more runs this morning to complete his 18th century. If he had got out soon after going in, the first Test might be over already and Australia 1-0 up.

Bell has played Test innings that have been physically

brave: when pounded by West Indies on a quick Oval pitch on his Test debut in 2004, or at the same ground in 2009 when he was pounded and hit several times by Mitchell Johnson.

But that was physical toughness. This was mental resolve – the resolve to hang in for the rest of the day, to be the specialist batsman that nursed England's tail, and to be the man who shaped the result of this critical opening Test.

Bell had also contributed hugely to the famous rearguard draws against South Africa at Cape Town and against New Zealand at Auckland last winter, without quite finishing the job. Graeme Onions and Matt Prior, respectively, had to man the last ditch.

Here Bell has surely completed the job, giving England a lead of 261 runs on a too-dry track, turning the tide with Matt Prior, then ramming home the advantage in his century partnership with Stuart Broad.

The mental resolve was manifest in Bell's determination to play straight in defence. Kevin Pietersen had shown how right-handers how to bat in these subcontinental conditions, more akin to Calcutta than Nottingham, and Bell followed his lead when playing himself in. It was only when he tried to score that he aimed square of, or behind, the wicket.

For rather too much of his England career, it could be said, Bell followed the lead in the wrong sort of way: by making his Test century after somebody else in the batting order had done so first. It was not until his tenth century that Bell made one without a team-mate getting to the landmark earlier in the match, and then it was against Bangladesh. But not here.

The all-round stroke play that has always been the hallmark of his batting, when coupled with his mental resolve, enabled Bell to find his way of scoring runs – except against Shane Watson, who did a fair impersonation of James Anderson when in a grumpy mood and down on pace, and who throttled every England batsman with his accuracy.

Born and bred before the Twenty20 age, Bell had the touch to cut bowlers quicker than Watson past slip. It is a stroke almost killed by Twenty20 – the proper cut, when the bat comes down on the ball from a horizontal position, not a dab or steer.

Bell did play the open-faced steer, the one which has been his downfall in the past when his resolve has weakened and he has sought a get-out clause.

But it was not until he had scored 77, and there had been something of a distraction in the previous over when Broad had edged Ashton Agar via the keeper to slip. Not since Dominic Cork decided to replace the bails and bat on, after hitting his wicket during the Old Trafford Test of 1995, has an England batsman been so brazen in shrugging off a dismissal.

It was not in the Spirit of Cricket of course, but it was in the Ashes tradition, and of Dr WG Grace replacing the bails after hitting his wicket and blaming the wind.

A more egotistic batsman than Bell would have accelerated thereafter to reach the personal glory of his 18th century before the close, but Broad was attempting high-risk shots after his reprieve and Bell decided not to rock the boat, and to grind Australia further down.

Bell also sat on Agar when the 19-year-old returned to his day-job.

The left-arm spinner bowled well against England's left-handers, dismissing Cook and Broad to all intents, as well as Jonny Bairstow when he pushed naively at a ball landing outside off stump and turning away.

Bell, however, was not troubled by Agar or anyone else. To the crisis he reacted superbly. And his impact will not be felt here alone, for if Australia lose this game after being on top following Agar's innings, their team-bus will have some demoralised passengers when it pulls into Lord's on Thursday.

Day Four
July 14 Scyld Berry

Australia (174-6 & 280) trail England (215 & 375) by 137 runs

Unless there is a second intervention of miraculous proportions by their 19-year-old debutant Ashton Agar, Australia will not score the 137 more runs they need to win the opening Ashes Test.

England have more battle-hardened warriors, and more self-belief, than their more youthful opponents. England also have two umpiring reviews left, Australia none, and that in itself is a major advantage in a low-scoring match. Accidents happen in the heat – although both on-field umpires are from hot countries – and England can rectify them this morning, as Alastair Cook has used his reviews as judiciously as his predecessor Andrew Strauss did, whereas Australia have used up their two.

Cook also has the option of taking a second new ball after nine more overs but he is unlikely to take it so quickly as Michael Clarke.

The game was on a knife edge, slicing and dicing nerves, until Clarke's decision on Friday afternoon played into the hands of Ian Bell, Matt Prior and Stuart Broad, who powered England ahead until the target was 311 – and 283 is the highest successful run-chase ever at Nottingham. England this morning will rely on the reverse-swing of James Anderson and Broad, and on the spin of Graeme Swann to see them home. Trent Bridge has been Swann's most unproductive Test ground, as it does not dust and disintegrate, but he persevered like a master craftsman to take the last two of the five wickets that England took.

And even if Agar performs a second miracle, England will at least have the consolation of going to Lord's with far more batsmen inducted into this series than Australia have. All of England's top eight have reached 30 and Ian Bell, with the utmost maturity, has made the only century.

Bell, 95 overnight, reached his 18th Test century in the opening minutes of day four when Australia's wheels came off. A beamer from Mitchell Starc went for five no-balls and a misfield saw Bell to only his second hundred against Australia, as the grinding-down process begun by Cook and Kevin Pietersen bore fruit.

But perhaps the highlight of England's innings on Saturday

was the standing ovation given to Stuart Broad when he reached 50, his first since the Abu Dhabi Test of 18 months ago, and again when he returned to the pavilion.

It was his home crowd, true, but they were in no doubt that he had taken the right, pragmatic course in standing his ground, even though he had hit the leather off the ball in edging it to slip.

When Australia embarked on their target of 311, they set off brightly, as they were bound to do. They were only going to slow down when the ball aged, and the target came on their horizon, and hope turned into the weight of expectation.

Chris Rogers and Shane Watson raised an opening bid of 28 by lunch at four runs an over, and of 84 by afternoon drinks. The heavy roller had been applied at Clarke's request, and not only to the pitch, so it seemed, but to the crowd, which became anxiously silent.

One of the first changes that Darren Lehmann made was to restore Watson to opening after the previous think tank thought it would be a good idea if he came in to bat in India when there was no pace on the ball. It was an obvious pairing: the attacking right-hander and accumulating left-hander in Rogers, but it still had to be enacted.

Clouds built up during Australia's opening stand, as if a storm was brewing – as there will be if England cannot defend 311 on such a parched pitch. Only three countries have chased down 200 in Nottingham, and none 300.

Drinks must have been tonics, or at least they served as such for England. For Watson they proved a distraction; and his concentration in a Test match has only twice lasted so long as five hours.

Watson planted his front foot as usual to play the first ball after the drinks break to leg, and missed it. It reverse-swung in a lot, so much that Watson asked for Aleem Dar's decision to be reviewed, but not too much. Only four Test batsmen have been lbw a higher proportion of times.

In Saturday's heat a tin roof was no place to be, yet Ed Cowan batted as if he was on one, as well as a king pair. Cook helped him, though – Cowan, after all, had written in a book that Cook was 'the most unaffected and lovely cricketer I have met throughout my career' – by taking off Broad after a spell of only five overs in which he got the ball to reverse nicely, and replacing him with Steve Finn, equally short of confidence and of a length.

Cowan was offered a cut for four by Finn and took it, and a couple of fours off Swann as he dropped short. But Cook knew of an off-spinner who could work the oracle: Root, who came on at the Radcliffe Road end, which Swann had not tried, and landed in the rough an off-break which Cowan edged to slip by means of an extravagant drive.

Rogers tends to fall across his crease. England had on occasion aimed full at his leg stump, but after tea Anderson tried a variation on this theme with a slower ball which Rogers chipped to midwicket. Australia had lost their anchor. England's supporters found their voice with 'O Jimmy, Jimmy!'

Clarke came in at No 4. It sounds simple but Clarke has found batting in this position anything but simple. He could bat in his favoured position of No 5 if only he had a senior to bat above him, but no Husseys or Pontings remain.

Clarke therefore has a major decision before Lord's: No 4, where his Test average has now sunk from 22 to 21, or down to five, promoting another callow youth ahead of him?

Broad dismissed Clarke with a ball he faintly edged. Clarke tried a review, perhaps in the knowledge that edges on a hot day show up less distinctly on Hot Spot, but the ploy did not work and Australia's last review was gone.

Australia had reached halfway to their target with only three wickets down. But their mountain suddenly turned into a landslide as they lost not only their captain but Steve Smith and Phil Hughes for only three runs.

Swann was so animated by the departure of Clarke that he started spinning the ball harder than in his previous 20 overs. He came up with a couple of rippers: both pinned the batsman on the back foot, the right-handed Smith and – after England had asked for a review of Kumar Dharmasena's decision – the left-handed Hughes. Game over, if Agar wills.

July 14 Steve James

Was it as much about the player as the principle? Was it the fact that it was Stuart Broad who did not walk on Friday that helped stir such a frenzied reaction?

These might seem strange questions, but then I found it an unfathomable response to a truly appalling piece of umpiring from Aleem Dar. Broad's demeanour can irritate. There is little doubt about that. But I have a suspicion that he was perceived as just the cocky upstart for some to pour forth their sanctimonious views on the Spirit of Cricket.

I don't recall there being such an outcry against Mike Atherton when he did not walk on this same ground against South Africa in 1998. In fact, the following passage of play involving numerous Allan Donald thunderbolts has since entered dreamy folklore.

What made Broad's stand so different from any of the other hundreds of occasions on which a batsman has not walked in recent times? Some have said because it was more blatant.

Well, that it is tosh. An edge is an edge – or in Atherton's case, a glove – and any batsman knows that, even if Michael Clarke appeared to deny that late in the day on Saturday when reviewing a feather edge he had got to, yes you guessed it, Broad.

I was a walker, doing so in two of my four Test innings, which, as one wag in the press box here at Trent Bridge pointed out on Saturday, is probably why I didn't do very well.

So, of course, I would prefer it if all batsmen walked, but the reality is that they don't. Unless everyone walks, it just won't work. Professional sports people will do what they can to win. That's what Clarke was doing last night.

This is an argument that really should have been put to bed a long time ago. People need to get over it.

I think Broad relished it. He is by some distance England's

feistiest cricketer. To have enraged the Australians will not have bothered him one jot. For it is part of the deal of not walking that you then cop mountains of abuse from the opposition. That is the reason some more timid folk walk. That was why I walked.

But Broad thrives on that sort of antagonism, that sort of red-blooded mood. Sometimes he has taken that too far and he has landed himself in hot water – for instance, he was fined half of his match fee for throwing the ball at Pakistan's Zulqarnain Haider in 2010 – but it appears that in general he has learnt to channel the excesses of that behaviour.

One only had to witness the ovation he received when striding out to bat yesterday morning to recognise the affection in which he held by his home crowd here. They certainly did not think he had done some grave disservice to the game, as had been suggested.

And neither did the cricketing gods, apparently, as Broad edged James Pattinson between first and second slips to bring up his fifty. Broad made 65 before edging the same bowler behind to Brad Haddin. Did he walk? Impossible to tell because the umpire's finger was raised so swiftly. He certainly did not linger.

But he had made valuable runs. He has not made as many as he should have in recent times, as opposition have probed a possible weakness against the short ball – many tall men have struggled in that respect.

And so England will have hoped those runs would bring wickets. That is often the way for all-rounders or bowlers-who-can-bat, to categorise Broad a little more accurately.

It had been the case when Broad had taken his stupendous seven for 44 against New Zealand at Lord's earlier this season. He had only made 26 not out, but it was amidst some latter-order chaos.

It did not do so initially, but it was little surprise when Broad made the breakthrough, trapping Shane Watson lbw as he played across his front pad. He was bowling from the Radcliffe Road End rather than the Pavilion End, from which he took a stunning hat-trick against India in 2011, but that was because Graeme Swann had to try to utilise the rough bowling from there.

Immediately, Swann had Chris Rogers given out. It was overturned on review, but it was noticeable how Broad had instantly altered the atmosphere with his spikiness. And so again later when getting Clarke, as Swann then mopped up Steve Smith and Phil Hughes.

I'd always have Broad in my team. And England enjoy having him in theirs right now. Off the field he is popular, and is especially close to Matt Prior, to whose son, Johnny, he is godfather.

In his recent book, *The Gloves are Off*, to which I may have lent a hand, Prior admits impressions can be misleading; that when he first saw Broad on TV making his international one-day debut he thought 'What a ponce!' But soon they were in the National Academy squad together and becoming best mates. 'The thing about Stu is that, yes, he has all the good looks, but the guy works bloody hard at his cricket,' said Prior, 'He is such a genuine bloke.'

I think he is.

Broad did not send cricket descending into anarchy on Friday. Cricketers know the boundaries concerning what is right or wrong, and, like it or not, his action on Friday did not cross any such line.

Day Five
July 15 Derek Pringle

England (215 & 375) beat Australia (296 & 280) by 14 runs

With a riveting Test match sending players and spectators into sensory overload on the final morning of drama, was it any wonder that James Anderson did not hear the inside edge he induced from Brad Haddin when Australia needed 15 runs to win the opening Ashes Test?

Fortunately for England, Hot Spot and the stump microphones were able to pick up and confirm the suspicions of Alastair Cook and Matt Prior, whose appeal and subsequent review brought this incredible Test match to a happy conclusion for the home side.

Fate always made it likely that technology would have the last say, given its strong influence on the match. That final process seemed to take an age, though. Finally, with 11 England fielders, two Australian batsmen and 16,000 spectators gazing at the giant replay screen, Aleem Dar changed his original decision and Anderson, after one premature celebration with team-mates, set off with arms splayed wide to celebrate England's victory.

Although the slim margin of England's win does not suggest a yawning gulf in quality between these two sides, in one respect – the use of technology – England were way ahead. Cook may still be learning his trade as a Test captain but he outsmarted Michael Clarke at every turn in this Test with his use of the Decision Review System (DRS), something Clarke had the grace to accept afterwards.

England have not won the opening Test of an Ashes series since 1997, when they beat Australia at Edgbaston, and they came close to missing out again after Haddin's courageous innings on a nerve-shredding final day took the Australians to within 16 runs of victory.

Brought back into the Test team to reprise the spirit of the Aussie battler, Haddin came within a couple of his favourite sweep slogs of playing the innings of his life. Australia do not revere glorious failure as much as the English but you could still make an argument for his 71 yesterday being the best innings of the match.

If he deserved better than to be microprocessed by the TV umpire, it was fitting that Anderson should be the man to benefit. But for his four wickets yesterday, Australia's journey from rank outsiders to near favourites would have produced a very different outcome to the one that sees England one-nil up with four Tests to play.

England began the final day with four wickets to take and a cushion of 137 runs, a position that few felt Australia could upset. But that confidence began to wane as Haddin and Ashton Agar began to settle and it was only after the second new ball, taken after 82 overs with Australia on 191 for six, that Anderson rebooted English optimism when he dismissed Agar, Mitchell Starc and Peter Siddle in the space of 24 balls.

Trent Bridge is Anderson's favourite ground and – come cloud or sun, quick pitch or slow – he always gets wickets here. Indeed, with his man-of-the-match 10 for 158 swelling his haul, he has taken more wickets in Tests at the ground than any other bowler. A total of 49 taken at 17.5 runs a wicket is a testament to his ability to find swing whatever the conditions.

To get his team within sight of the prize, Cook bowled Anderson for 13 successive overs in the opening session yesterday. With the second Test at Lord's just three days away, it seemed a gamble worth taking given the prize on offer. Cook might have hastened the process had he been more aggressive with his field settings and given Anderson two slips to the tail-enders rather than one. But having dropped a catch off Siddle, when he was on 10, he then caught a blinder diving to his right in Anderson's next over when Siddle flashed again.

Cook was bold to take the new ball. With the old one offering reverse-swing and grip for the spinner, as well as being more difficult for the batsmen to time, some captains would have continued on as they were. But the new ball, with its hard seam, penetrated the fissures more easily as well bouncing more off uncracked areas to give a greater variation of bounce than the old ball, which spreads more on impact.

Still, it did not happen straight away and Anderson had to wait until his third over with the new ball before he got the steep bounce that accounted for Agar, who edged to Cook at slip. At that point, Australia still needed 104 to win, an unlikely achievement that looked more distant when Starc also edged to Cook in a reprise of his first innings dismissal, pushing hard at one that Anderson ran across him.

If a home win looked a formality, then Siddle struck a familiarly defiant pose by striking a brace of fours as he and Haddin added 20 in 37 balls.

With 80 required, Anderson dismissed him too, but that simply sparked Haddin, who began to chance his arm with some big shots – mostly against Steve Finn, whom he struck for three fours in successive balls to bring up his fifty. Cook only risked him for two overs, a situation that puts his place in jeopardy for the next Test on Thursday.

With Australia nine wickets down, the lunch break was extended for 30 minutes or until the last wicket fell. It is a new playing condition and yesterday it favoured Australia, given that Anderson had just retired to the dressing-room to get a bout of cramp sorted and James Pattinson was playing with all the aplomb of the opening batsman that his 14-year-old self used to be.

As a result Cook slowed things down, though when Broad farcically removed his boot and insole in order to ensure his was the last over before lunch, Kumar Dharmasena insisted there would be one more despite the clock indicating 1.30pm.

With Australia requiring 20 to win, the teams returned from the break to Sean Ruane, the opera singer, belting out Danny Boy, Rule Britannia and Land of Hope and Glory, in a bid to stir the capacity crowd. It was cheesy patriotism but it seemed to work and amid the ensuing chorus of 'Oh Jimmy

Jimmy', the Terror of Trent Bridge struck with his 11th ball after lunch to give England first blood in the series.

July 15 Simon Hughes

Michael Holding, the West Indies fast bowler who was known as 'Whispering Death', has a good yardstick for judging bowlers. Only when one has taken at least four wickets-per-Test over a long period of time, can they be considered 'great'.

Of quick bowlers Fred Trueman managed it, and so did Australia's Glenn McGrath, the irrepressible New Zealander Richard Hadlee and the exceptional West Indian Malcolm Marshall.

With his 10 wickets, Jimmy Anderson nudged closer to that milestone. He now has 317 wickets in 83 Tests. He is on the verge of greatness.

Anderson's second 10-wicket haul at Trent Bridge was very different from his first three years ago, against Pakistan, and illustrates how much he has developed in that time.

Those wickets were mostly top-order players dismissed using lavish, conventional swing with the new, or newish ball. Here virtually all his wickets were achieved by making a roughed up ball move one way or another.

This has been the major enhancement in his game – finding just enough movement in the air or off the surface with an older ball and utilising it brilliantly.

In that sense he is peerless. No one else has his range of skills and adaptability, nor given his 13-over spell on Sunday morning, his stamina.

He cruised into bowl for an hour and a half, unwaveringly, unstintingly, with metronomic accuracy. In those 13 overs he conceded only three boundaries, and two of those were off the edge, as he probed away relentlessly around off-stump, insistent with his questioning of the batsman's technique.

Like the great Hadlee – a similar style of bowler to Anderson – he is an indefatigible examiner.

Hadlee once said that an over was like having six bullets in a gun and you used each bullet strategically to get your opponent into a vulnerable position before nailing him.

Since Anderson has teamed up with England's bowling coach David Saker, you can see him doing that.

On day four Anderson was moving the left-handed Chris Rogers around the crease, drawing him across his stumps with a succession of balls curving away delivered from round the wicket, trying to get him overbalancing and pinning him lbw with one that went the other way.

Eventually he got him with a cutter that had the same effect, causing him to chip a catch to midwicket as he fell over. Anderson signalled acknowledgement to Saker after that wicket.

On the final day, he immediately struck up a superb rhythm and began nagging away incessantly at Brad Haddin's resolve. The pitch had gone to sleep, but there was just enough reverse swing to keep him watchful.

Anderson swung a few away, Haddin was resolutely behind them. He tried the odd inswinger. Haddin, hanging on the back foot fearing lbws, playing the ball as late as possible, defiantly kept them out. He gave him nothing to hit.

The ball he eventually dismissed Ashton Agar with was superbly contrived, as it was proceeded by inswingers from round the wicket, forcing him to play, then a ball that was angled in on the same line but curved away and drew a fatal prod to one he could have left.

Reverse swing permits this kind of precise interrogation. It is more controllable than conventional swing. Once the ball is in the required state, you know as a bowler it will go the way you intend, and usually the degree too. Normal – ie new ball – swing is far less well behaved.

It is like a supermarket trolley. It has a mind of its own. Unless your release is exactly right, the seam in a perfect position, conventional swing is highly unco-operative. Start it on off stump and it will go. Start it on leg stump and it will not.

Anderson is at the forefront of England's ball management as they strive to get one side as worn and ragged as possible.

He is the one mainly bowling wobble-seam deliveries that land by the side of the seam rather than on it, he is the one who shies at the stumps from mid-on, deliberately bouncing the ball in the dirt around the wicket-ends, it is he who cradles the ball delicately between his thumb and forefinger as he is polishing it to avoid getting his sweaty palms on the parched leather.

On dry pitches, reverse swing is actually a more dangerous weapon than spin when employed by an operator as slick as Anderson. Graeme Swann will happily concede that.

He was, of course, indebted to the fielders for his

match-winning performance, not just Alastair Cook's slip catching but Ian Bell's agility, too.

Twice he dived at extra cover and prevented a single to Haddin. It was this that persuaded him to chase a slightly wider length ball with a hint of inswing that induced the crucial edge.

He had taken all four of the wickets England required in 15 flawless overs at a personal cost of just 29.

Anderson might not be a 'great' quite yet, but, green pitch or bare, he has become, for Australia, Public Enemy No1.

July 15 Geoffrey Boycott

The reason England won was because they are more battle-hardened than Australia. We have plenty of individuals who can stand up and perform under pressure.

You need batsmen and bowlers who can be mentally strong and do not freeze at the big moments.

England were that team. Australia had their chances and were not good enough to grasp the nettle. They have shown fight and at times the match swung in their favour. When Ashton Agar came to the crease at 117 for nine in the first innings they were 108 behind England and when he got out he had given them a 65-run lead with a breathtaking innings.

The Australian seamers then had England rocking at 131 for four with only a 64-run lead. But they could not find their killer instinct. I fear that is what is going to happen through-out this series.

The Australians will fight and scrap and have a number of opportunities but I do not see enough quality in the overall individuals to beat England, in England, in a series. There are moments in all Tests when either side can grab the initiative and go on to win. But you have to be good enough to take it. I do not think this Australian team are.

England had individuals who took their chances. After England failed in their first innings by making only 215 there was an extra burden on the bowlers and James Anderson delivered his best with five wickets.

In England's second innings Kevin Pietersen and Ian Bell had to change their normal batting tempo. They cut out the expansive shots, were prepared to be patient to stay in and not go looking for the boundaries. They made sure they forced the bowlers to bowl to them and mentally had the experience and class to adapt to the situation.

Bell played his most important innings for England. It set up an England win. Every batsman likes scoring hundreds but they matter more when it wins the match. Centuries on flat batting pitches or when the game is a draw do not mean as much.

Then it is just a nice statistic and you should never judge any cricketer by statistics alone. Bell's patient, skilful batting was a delight to watch. His composure, judgment of length, sureness of footwork and exquisite timing were a joy to behold.

On the final day with the pressure mounting again Anderson delivered. Without Jimmy, England would not have won, as Graeme Swann was not at his best. He either bowled too straight or too full and he does not have a good record at Trent Bridge. Broad was good but he did not have Jimmy's penetration or wicket-taking ability.

Steven Finn was so poor that Cook did not have confidence in him. He bowled 10 overs in the second innings, Swann bowled 44 and Anderson 32. That tells you everything. I cannot see Finn keeping his place for Lord's. If the captain does not have the confidence to bowl you in a four-man attack then you are struggling.

There has been a lot of claptrap about Stuart Broad not walking. Throughout the history of cricket there have been moments like the Broad decision and some defined the attitude between the two teams for the rest of the series.

Even the great Don Bradman was accused by the England players of not walking and Wisden records it as such. In the first Test at Brisbane in 1946 he nicked Bill Voce to Jack Ikin at second slip. He was given not out and made 187.

Walter Hammond, the England captain, made the famous comment to him: 'Is that how we are going to play cricket in this series then?' Australia won by an innings and won the series 3-0.

Then there is the Mike Atherton-Allan Donald incident here in 1998. It was as blatant a glove to the wicketkeeper as you will ever see. I played in the second Test at Melbourne in 1965 when Doug Walters was going for his second Test hundred in his second match. The game was petering out for a draw and we were saving the bowlers' energy so I was bowling. He hit it straight back to me, caught and bowled. He was given not out.

The 'spirit of cricket' was Colin Cowdrey's concept when

he was chairman of the International Cricket Council. He prided himself on being a walker. And he was – when he got a century and could return to the dressing room to great applause.

The test of walking is when you have single figures and you touch it. Can you go when you are a failure? I have seen human nature at work. Most fail the moral test, Cowdrey included.

So no more rubbish about walking. The only way is for nobody to walk. Leave it to the umpires. The laws of the game say 'in the umpire's opinion'. The only reason most of us turn and go without waiting for the umpire's decision when we nick it to slip is because it is so obvious it would be embarrassing to stand our ground. Broad was not embarrassed. Good luck to him.

The final word. Richie Benaud is regarded as a great cricketer, great captain and iconic commentator. He did the first reading of the Cowdrey Lecture. He said: 'Australians never walk. They are taught not to walk.' That sums it up.

July 16 Michel Vaughan

Alastair Cook will not have slept well on Sunday night. The emotion and relief after such a draining match with a tense finish leaves the brain clicking over every decision you made when you finally get to bed.

The match at Trent Bridge is the closest I have seen to the Test we won against Australia by two runs in 2005 at Edgbaston. I know from my experience that the closer Australia got to their target on Sunday a sense of panic would have been welling up inside Cook. He hid it well behind those sunglasses. I did the same. But like me he will have been absolutely panicking, blaming himself for decisions he made and thinking: 'We will never get these guys out.'

I have always said that you have to be a good actor to be the England captain and Cook did well on Sunday by hiding his emotions. He sent a calm, positive message to the rest of the team. Inside it would have been very different.

The comparisons with Edgbaston 2005 hit me on Sunday when Australia trimmed the target to 100 with two wickets in hand. That was the number they required on the start of the Sunday at Edgbaston.

When he took that brilliant catch at slip off Peter Siddle, Cook will have breathed a huge sigh of relief. He would have looked at James Pattinson and sized him up against Graeme Swann and James Anderson and thought it would be all over in a few minutes. You start planning how you are going to celebrate. Will I go mad and jump all over the place or act cool? You think: 'Great we are going 1-0 up.'

He then turned to Steven Finn. Cook must have thought he would give him a confidence boost by taking the winning wicket. Finn then goes to Lord's happy and everything is right in the team.

But as soon as the Australians went after Finn, Cook would have thought: 'What have I done?' He made a decision out of sentiment. He tried to give a boost to a struggling young kid. I like that because it is important to look after your players but Cook did the right thing by hauling him off.

He brought back Stuart Broad but the runs were being

chipped away and that is when he will have experienced that sick feeling I had in 2005. It is horrible to think you are going to lose such a historic match from a massive position of strength. As captain you are the one who will take the blame.

He would have thought: Did I keep Jimmy going for too long and ruin him for the next Test? Alternatively, should I have kept Jimmy on for longer to get the last wicket? Was Finn's catch in the deep our last opportunity? Should I have put a different fielder there? Have I got enough slips? Should I put a man on the drive? Help.

The one thing I realised on Sunday is that it is a lot easier being out in the middle. I found commentating on a close finish much more nerve-racking than playing. I asked Mark Nicholas if this is what it felt like in 2005. He said it was worse. How did we cope? It is amazing that players produce their skills under such pressure. But they are so focused. They do not hear the crowd. They concentrate on each ball as a moment in time.

Cook will have been praying: 'Just let the ball hit a crack in the pitch, play a horror shot. Give us something.' Every time Pattinson played a forward defensive with such a straight bat he would have thought: 'We're done here.'

You never see that vital wicket until it happens. In 2005 I could not see how we would get Brett Lee or Michael Kasprowicz out. They were playing well and the ball was not moving. In the end we were a little lucky. The same on Sunday: Haddin was caught behind off an inside edge. It is not often they go to the keeper.

The lunch break came at the right time. The Edgbaston

match was over before lunch but England had that little breather. It slowed the game down and it was at that point Australia realised how close they were to winning. Cook had to turn to his best two bowlers after lunch. Swann and Anderson were not going to bowl any pies. Australia had to work for their runs. All of a sudden 20 runs felt like 200 to the last pair. When you are miles from a target you play with freedom. When you get within touching distance the pressure starts to weigh. One mistake loses the game.

The big difference to 2005 was that if we had lost that match we would have been 2-0 down and dead and buried. England only played in third gear at Trent Bridge. They can move up to new levels. In 2005 when we lost the opening Test at Lord's we took the positives out of it: we bowled Australia out twice, none of them made a hundred, KP was good on debut and we were proactive. Australia have to do the same. The question from Trent Bridge will be how much damage has it done to Australia? Lose at Lord's and they are 2-0 down. There is no coming back from that.

Cook will have been thinking over all these things lying awake on Sunday night. He will have been looked ahead to Thursday. Which team do we pick? How do I improve my field settings for each bowler? Can we improve our plans to the Aussie batters?

He will see the team analyst on Tuesday who will help with those things but I think a captain has to write it all down himself. It triggers the mind and is a reference book for later. Anyone can come up with new tricks but a captain only learns by committing it to paper.

Second Test Lords Day One
July 19 Derek Pringle

England (289-7) v Australia

The Queen visited Lord's to meet both teams and stayed for an hour, long enough to see England slump to 28 for three. Had she stayed all day she might have been tempted to knight Ian Bell on the spot after he scored his second century of the series and his third in successive Ashes Tests.

A packed and sweltering Lord's rose to acclaim him, full of admiration. They had been roasting for six hours just watching so they marvelled at how easy he made it all look. If his hundred at Trent Bridge was made under more pressure, this was easier on the eye, which is what the faithful here prefer.

It also got England out of a pickle, his 144-run partnership with Jonny Bairstow, and his 99-run one with Jonathan Trott before that, helping to nose their team in front until Steve Smith, a latecomer into the action, dismissed them both as well as Matt Prior with his leg-breaks, to allow Australia to shade the day.

England, who finished on 289 for seven, will want to get around 350 on Friday, a target they obviously feel within their reach after sending out a nightwatchman, James Anderson, to protect a No 9, Stuart Broad. It surprised everybody, not least the Aussie supporters who, assuming it was Broad, began to boo.

Bell has scored hundreds in clusters before so he has not just discovered gluttony. He made three in three Tests against Pakistan in 2006 and five hundreds in eight Tests in 2010-11, when he was arguably England's best batsman. He then endured something of a slump until now when that trio of successful batting – confidence, concentration and sublime timing – have become perfectly aligned like heavenly bodies.

Some batsmen strike the ball but Bell just seems to ease it around as Colin Cowdrey and Tom Graveney used to do. Some of his back-foot shots through the covers defined aesthetics, and defied physics, the minimal fuss at the bat face belying the speed with which they raced to the boundary. It is why more poetry has been written about batting than any other sporting discipline.

If this looked like confirmation of a new ruthless Bell, he lapsed into his old casual self soon after reaching his hundred. In what many accredit to Michael Clarke's innovative captaincy, but what was actually a last resort, Smith was brought into the attack to bowl his wrist-spin. A few pies ensued, one a full toss that Bell despatched over mid-on for four, but when Smith landed and turned one from a good length, Bell was a tad loose in defending and edged to slip.

The move to bowl Smith then looked a masterstroke as he caught and bowled Jonny Bairstow for 67, the batsman miscuing a low full toss. Australians, as well as bowlers everywhere, will consider it poetic justice that Bairstow did not go on to reach his maiden Test hundred.

Clean-bowled by Peter Siddle when on 21, he was reprieved when TV replays showed that the bowler had failed, by about a millimetre, to ground some part of his heel behind the back edge of the front crease. On a hot day and on a flat pitch, when a fast bowler knocks over your stumps but has overstepped by such a minute margin it is morally out, though so far in this series only England appear to have benefited when the cricketing ethics have gone awry.

Smith then took his third wicket when he had Prior caught behind trying to force a back-foot shot through the covers. Aggression is the game Prior peddles but with five overs to go, it was a poor shot. Since he was named England's Player of the Year, Prior's Test scores have been nought, nought, 39, four not out, one, 31 and six.

Alastair Cook had probably not planned on having Prior out or even in by the close of play after he had won the toss and batted on another scorching summer's day. But like England, who had dropped Steven Finn for Tim Bresnan, Australia made changes to their side, the most significant being the inclusion of Ryan Harris for Mitchell Starc, possibly because right-arm pace bowlers tend to bowl better on the Lord's slope than left.

Harris almost qualified for England on the basis of a British passport in 2008, when he almost declared himself a home player for Sussex, but was persuaded otherwise by Queensland, where he lived.

On Thursday, he bowled like a veteran, probing just the right line and length from the Pavilion end to have Joe Root lbw and Kevin Pietersen caught behind, the first coming down the slope the other staying up it. It was a one-two Glenn McGrath used to exploit better than anyone, which is why Australia had him advise them recently.

Root, who had seen his captain fall lbw to Shane Watson (Clarke's first masterstroke when he had him replace James Pattinson after just two overs), reviewed the decision but after lengthy consideration and numerous replays, Tony Hill, the TV umpire, decided that the ball had struck pad just before bat – there were Hot Spot marks on both – and Root had to go.

Pietersen came and went, quickly, his nibble at one he probably had to play at ending in a fine edge to Brad Haddin. His exit left England reeling at 28 for three, with a rout in prospect before Trott then Bell settled the crowd with a solid partnership of which Trott made the lion's share.

A big score beckoned for Trott until Harris banged one in short and he shovelled it to Usman Khawaja at deep square-leg, a mistake that gave the deserving Harris a third wicket and the even more deserving Bell an unfettered platform on which to score his 19th Test hundred.

July 19 Scyld Berry

Persistently these Australians fail to follow the script – England's script, that is.

They are allowed to take three of England's wickets with the new ball in the opening hour, if they must, but not to take three more in the last hour with occasional wrist-spin.

England's script had Ian Bell and Jonny Bairstow coming

together at 127 for four and batting through the rest of the day for unbeaten centuries, ending it with the same regal splendour that it had begun.

And the Great Reprieve when Bairstow was bowled by Peter Siddle, only for the television umpire Tony Hill to call no-ball, was meant to have been the moment when the door was finally shut on Australia's chance of regaining the Ashes.

Bairstow had scored 21, and England were afloat at 172-4 after Hill's call, rather than capsizing at 171-5.

But England did not kick on towards the total that would have insulated them against any chance of defeat in this game and any realistic prospect of losing the Ashes: neither side has come from behind to win the last three Tests of a series in England.

England, as unpalatable fact, have not batted well all year. Nobody has scored a big hundred and therefore England have not scored 500.

Even in India before Christmas, England did not bat well as a unit. Their match-winning totals were largely monuments personally built by Alastair Cook.

Some precious ingredient has gone missing since 2011 when England batted India and, before them, Australia into submission. Since Andrew Strauss retired, the ratio of six right-handers to one left-hander has not been ideal, but it is more the tone that has changed.

When England were piling up their huge totals against India and Australia, their batting smacked of earnest endeavour. They built brick by brick, ran their singles hungrily, and looked to go up gradually through the gears.

But on the first day of this series at Trent Bridge, England's batsmen responded to the heat much as their supporters did. It was slip, slap, slop: a thick-edged drive to slip, a slap to cover, and a general sloppiness in trying to hit boundaries from the outset.

There were echoes in their first innings here – which is why Bell and Bairstow came together when only 33 overs had been bowled on a pluperfect pitch, and England were on the verge of squandering the massive advantage of winning the toss.

Bairstow is not yet a complete batsman, like Bell in his maturity. He seems rather more, not less, bottom-handed than he was last summer, which he ended by batting as imperiously as Kevin Pietersen in the drawn Lord's Test against South Africa.

One could argue that Bairstow should have been given the whole of England's series in New Zealand to groove his game – in the eventuality, predictable by then, that Joe Root would open instead of Nick Compton against Australia.

It would have been hard on Bell to be dropped, but he would have been reinstated as soon as Kevin Pietersen was injured.

Then Bairstow would have had time to iron out the wrinkles in his batting: after a series of facing the left-arm spin of Bruce Martin, he might not have succumbed to a push at Ashton Agar at Trent Bridge.

Against pace it is the premature closing of the bat's face that is Bairstow's flaw. Plenty of Test batsmen have a predilection for midwicket, but Cook and Trott do not close the face as soon as Bairstow did when bowled by Siddle.

July 19 Simon Hughes

Lord's is a capricious place for bowlers. It rewards consistency and punishes uncertainty. Men who are sure of their game and stick to it usually prevail.

Those who are striving for rhythm and confidence generally suffer. Such were the contrasting fortunes that befell Australia's opening pair of James Pattinson and Ryan Harris.

There are 10 years between them in age and a chasm on Thursday in expertise. Harris, 33, dismissed three of England's top four at a cost of just 43 and always threatened. Pattinson, 23, bowled 18 wicketless overs and conceded 78 runs.

He did not look like getting anybody out, even the nightwatchman Jimmy Anderson when armed with the second new ball. Such wayward performances test a captain's patience and imagination, and Michael Clarke will be thankful that the experiment with Steve Smith's leg spin was so successful.

He will rue not giving him a go in Nottingham at some stage.

Australia made the right call in selecting Harris. He is a man who keeps things simple. Asked if he considered himself a seam or swing bowler he said: 'I consider myself a fast bowler . . . well, medium-fast anyway.'

He is not concerned with grand descriptions of himself or elaborate means of taking wickets. He bustles in and propels the ball down at a decent lick, trying to bowl a repetitive line, and is confident in his ability to do so. He does not notice things like sloping pitches.

'We spoke to Glenn McGrath about that before the game and he advised us just to put the Lord's slope out of our minds and just imagine it as a flat pitch so that is what I tried to do. I didn't mind which end I bowled.'

In fact he bowled all his overs from the Pavilion End, including a probing first spell which brought him two wickets. First he dismissed Joe Root with a full delivery that nipped into him – the perfect ball to a batsman who likes to hang on the back foot – and then he added Kevin Pietersen in the same over.

Playing for movement down the slope, the ball instead held its line and took the edge as Pietersen tried to pull his bat out of the way. Later he noticed Jonathan Trott's habit of leaping onto the front foot almost before the ball had been delivered, dug one in and lured him into an uppish pull.

Pattinson, meanwhile, looked unsure of himself on Thursday as he had at Trent Bridge, where he was generally erratic. The burden of leading the Australian attack had weighed heavily.

It was not the state of mind to bring to a Lord's Test with its history and attention and unusual geography. The whole Lord's experience can be very daunting. There is the grandeur – the scale of the Pavilion, the famous names on the honours board, the legendary figures staring at you sternly from the paintings on the wall. There is the extra attention that the Home of Cricket attracts.

And then there is the slope. If you are too conscious of its presence it can be destabilising. You think about the different lines you need to bowl from one end to the other, the different ways a batsman may play at each end, the different fields you might set. You become acutely conscious of the angles, especially if you are generally struggling for control. And your natural rhythm is corrupted.

Pattinson's second ball of the match – from the Nursery End – was a friendly leg stump half volley to Alastair Cook, which was put away for four. The same thing happened to his ninth delivery. He barely made him play in between and was swiftly replaced by Shane Watson. Once Watson had trapped Cook lbw, Pattinson was brought back. There was no improvement. He had bowled four unproductive overs in two spells. Watson replaced him again.

Then he was put on at the Pavilion End. The required line from there is about a foot more to the off side than at the Nursery End. That just magnified his inaccuracy. He could hardly get two balls in the same place.

Even his bouncer looped harmlessly down the legside. It was hopeless. Lord's had claimed another victim. He will have headed to his bed last night glad to have found something private and flat.

Day Two

July 20 Derek Pringle

England (361 & 31-3) lead Australia (128) by 264 runs

Sir Ian Botham's reputation as a tipster lags well behind those he acquired with bat and ball, but his prediction of

10-0 double whitewash by England no longer looks like the ravings of a misguided patriot after another abject batting performance by Australia. In front of another full house at Lord's on another sparkling summer's day, Australia capitulated to 128 all out in conditions that simply screamed runs.

Then, when England decided to bat again rather than enforce the follow-on, they missed the chance of an early breakthrough when an edge by Joe Root off Shane Watson passed between first slip and the wicket-keeper.

It was a break England should have capitalised on to put the game beyond Australia, but as in the first Test, they struggled to summon the killer instinct, scarcely playing a shot save the slap to cover that did for Kevin Pietersen. Instead, Peter Siddle found a bustling rhythm from the Pavilion End to dismiss Alastair Cook, Jonathan Trott and Pietersen in the space of 16 balls to keep England, their lead extended to 264 by the close, just this side of the horizon.

Australia's batting was identified as their weak suit before this series began, though nobody suspected how bad it was until they were 117-9 in their first innings at Trent Bridge.

There they were rescued by a teenager making his debut and in the second innings by a veteran making a comeback, but that leaves a lot of dead wood in between, something turned gleefully into kindling on Friday by England's bowlers. It left Darren Lehmann, Australia's new coach, cutting a lone, disconsolate figure on the visitor's balcony, which looked like an isolation ward. Whatever the malaise he inherited with this team, the prospect of a cure seems a distant one.

There could be no excuses for Australia either, after Stuart Broad and Graeme Swann gave them a pointer as to how runs might be scored when they added 48 breezy runs in 40 balls for the last wicket. With Swann later taking five for 44, the visitors' surrender was so tame that England's continued possession of the Ashes looks as if it will happen with the minimum of fuss.

For anyone wanting the semblance of a contest it was a depressing display and its meekness made a case for Alastair Cook enforcing the follow-on. Although there was over-whelming logic to England batting again with the weather set fair, the bowlers in need of a recharge and a dusting pitch wearing by the session, Australia looked so shot as to be ripe for another rout.

The rot did not set in immediately, after the opening pair had added 42 without undue alarm. Shane Watson, a brilliant driver of the ball, had even looked dominant, talking 21 runs off two overs from James Anderson and Tim Bresnan.

But a switch to the Pavilion End for Bresnan saw him nip one down the slope into Watson planted front foot and win not just an lbw for himself but probably one for Swann too, after Watson reviewed, apparently at the insistence of Chris Rogers, an lbw that always looked dead.

With one review left Rogers seemed loath to request the other, when he missed a thigh high full toss from Swann after lunch. Had he done so, he would have been reprieved after Hawkeye had the ball missing the top of leg-stump. It was arguably the worst ball to get a wicket in Test history, though David Gower's dismissal of Kapil Dev for 116 in Kanpur

28 years ago was reputed to be pretty appalling. High full tosses can present problems when bowled by pace bowlers but Rogers should have been able to pick any spot on the leg-side boundary and hit it there.

England bowled as they mostly do, with discipline and skill, but this was no overwhelming force blowing away batsmen unable to cope with pace, swing or spin. The pitch is dusting in places, which allows the seam to grip occasionally for pace bowlers and spinners, but this is no minefield.

Having seen his rank full toss hit the jackpot, Swann wheeled away getting some to grip off the pitch and others to leap from the footholes. One theory why Mitchell Starc was left out of this match was that Australia's selectors feared the rough he might create from Swann.

With Bresnan luring Phillip Hughes into a wild slash and another wasted review by Australia, Swann was left to work his way through the remainder of the order. He began with Usman Khawaja, who looks a walking wicket providing you can keep him pegged down for an over or two. Dropped off Swann at slip by Trott, Khawaja never looked comfortable and his demise, caught by Pietersen after miscueing a lofted drive, was entirely predictable.

Steve Smith followed next, his technique of playing defensively with bat well in front of pad undone when the ball bounced more than expected to rebound off the splice into the hands of Ian Bell at short leg. Swann then deferred to Broad for the wicket of Clarke, lbw to one that flirted with hitting leg-stump but which, with no reviews left, Clarke could not query.

Ashton Agar, now seemingly permanently promoted to seven, tried to add responsibility to his repertoire but his pursuit of a quick leg bye was refused by Brad Haddin and made late enough to smell the burnt rubber as Prior's quick thinking and even quicker throw beat the teenager's hasty retreat to the bowler's end.

Although there did not appear to be much reverse-swing, Anderson made out as if the ball might be moving by covering it as he ran in to bowl. Whether Siddle was fooled or whether the ball that he edged to second slip simply bounced a bit more than the others was irrelevant, another wicket had gone.

Swann then mopped up the tail, though on a day when it was impossible to distinguish where Australia's top order ended and its lower one began, it was one of the more egalitarian five-wicket hauls on the famous Lord's boards.

July 20 Scyld Berry

It has been a poor series to date for the top-order batsmen of both countries. If Joe Root reaches 65 today, it will be the highest score by anybody in the top four of England or Australia.

But unproductive starts have been more of a problem for Australia. England have had Ian Bell at No 5 to anchor their innings, whereas Australia's batting – except for their last-wicket pairs – has been as short of solidity as an ice cream in this heatwave.

Australia's lack of a consistent opening batsman is also

a long-standing one, and a primary reason for their fall from grace. Conan Doyle's mysteries centred on Sherlock Holmes. This one centres on Watson – not Dr Watson but DRS Watson as he could be called after his latest recourse to the referral system.

How can such a brilliant stroke-player as Shane Watson – a master, nothing less, of the pull and front-foot drive – be so incapable of building an innings that he has only twice reached 60 in Tests since 2010?

This problem is aggravated, not alleviated, by his stroke-playing brilliance. If Watson scored his 30s and 40s slowly, like a traditional New Zealand opening batsman, he would hang around long enough to build his side's innings. By the time he had done his stuff, his side would have at least 100 on the board, and the ball would be ageing and softening.

Instead, Watson flies to his average Test score of 35. He dispatches half-a-dozen balls to the boundary, so that often the opening bowlers are still in their first spell by the time he has been dismissed – lbw, front foot planted, or else slicing a drive to slip.

Thus Watson has the same effect on Australia as caffeine. He is not so much a double-shot as a six-shot latte, who stimulates his team-mates until they reach a high, and think batting is simple, then gets out and leaves them deflated.

Mickey Arthur, the former coach, is said to have called Watson 'a cancer' in the Australian team because of his selfishness. He is the son of an air force pilot – a type renowned for acting as individuals – and seems to plot his own course, brief and glorious; but, above all, brief.

It is a far cry from predecessors like Justin Langer, Matthew Hayden and Simon Katich, who sweated buckets for the Australian team as opening batsmen. They could score quickly, but if conditions were harsh they would put on a hair-shirt, limit their strokes, and grind opposing bowlers into the dirt.

Katich is still churning out runs for Lancashire as a dogged left-hander, after being dropped by Australia at the end of 2010, a year in which he had already hit two centuries and four other scores of 79 or more. Between 'Katto' and 'Watto' the difference in time span is short, and in cricket culture immense.

In any other age of Australian cricket over the last century, Watson would have been dropped long ago for his failure to convert starts into substance. But in the T20 era he has been able to tease with twenties and thirties and retain his place, because his contemporaries have much the same defect, and they have not been able to bowl as a fourth seamer.

Phil Hughes? This prodigy – the youngest batsman to score two centuries in a Test, aged 20 – has yet to change his method sufficiently to cope with international cricket. Like so many promising English batsmen of the bad old days, he was selected when he should not have been, and will not be selected when he has developed his game and should be.

Usman Khawaja? A lost soul on the fringes, both in the field and dressing-room. David Warner? Well, he doesn't have to return to England from the Australia A tour of southern Africa as a reformed personality: scores of six and 11 against Zimbabwe A are surely enough for him to regain his Test place.

It is the same picture in Australia's domestic cricket: lots of good batsmen who can score quick 30s and attract IPL franchises, but no very good batsmen who can bat all day. The Sheffield Shield has been dumbed down like the county championship before splitting into two divisions, into low-scoring scraps on seaming pitches.

Only two batsmen scored as many as three centuries in the last Sheffield Shield, neither a nipper. And in the wake of Ricky Ponting and Chris Rogers, the four batsmen who hit two centuries included Phil Hughes and Brad Haddin.

So not much incentive for Watson to bat like his predecessors, discipline his shot-selection, think more of taking quick singles, or rotate the strike. If he keeps blazing away, however briefly, he is sure of his place for this series, and his IPL value will no doubt increase.

July 20 Paul Hayward

To restore the glorious tension of Trent Bridge last week the Ashes need Michael Clarke's side to stop donating their wickets to English bowlers and take time to read the manual on decision reviews.

If they carry on as they did on this second day at Lord's – where the great Australian players of yesteryear rounded on them for their self-destructive batting – Clarke and the rest of his top six will be broken by an England side whose own work with the willow is hardly imperious.

Alastair Cook's fall for eight as Australia returned to the field 233 runs behind reaffirmed that England's batters are also disjointed and underperforming.

Their only boast is that they are slightly less disjointed than Australia. Jonathan Trott and Kevin Pietersen soon joined Cook back in the Pavilion to leave England at 30 for three. All fell to Peter Siddle, who took three wickets for four runs in 16 balls. In Nottingham and here in London, England have owed their superiority at the crease to Ian Bell. Until Siddle's flourish, the 11 Australians beneath those baggy green caps seemed doomed to lose their sixth Test in a row: their worst run since 1984.

The small burst of spirit we saw in Thursday's opening session gave rise to a hope that this could be another classic series to match the summer corkers of 2005 and 2009. Ryan Harris brought fresh punching power to Australia's attack. Steve Waugh's pre-match campanology from the balcony was a clanging call to arms. The old legends filed off the bus like an international rescue squad. They gave their pep talks and took their seats in shirts and ties or worked their way through media rotas: Ricky Ponting, Shane Warne, Glenn McGrath and Adam Gilchrist were all on hand to inspire by example.

The first day ended with England 289-7 with Bell the saviour of some unconvincing batting. That total was inflated to 361 before Australia took up their cudgels, to great comedic effect. First, Shane Watson wastes a review on an lbw decision he had no chance of overturning. His error: playing across the line to a straight delivery. Then, Chris Rogers falls to a full-toss from Graeme Swann that was missing leg stump. His error: allowing Watson's ridiculous appeal to deter him from asking for his own review, which would have saved his wicket. Next: Phil Hughes drives at an angled Tim Bresnan ball and burns Australia's last review in a vain attempt to show he had not nicked the ball (he had).

So: Australia, 53 for three. Usman Khawaja then lofts a Swann delivery to Pietersen: another scatty stroke, which put the Australian innings in a spiral. Working down a list of silly ways to be dismissed, they then contrived a run-out for Ashton Agar, and soon England were scuttling them out for 128.

During lunch, Warne had been inducted into cricket's hall of fame in front of the Pavilion while the collapsing team of 2013 applauded from their balcony.

The shadow of the Ponting/Waugh years will not lift. When things are going well they hearten with their presence. When the day turns sour, they are the juxtaposition from hell. McGrath called Australia's batting 'horrendous' and 'unacceptable'. Warne diagnosed 'a lack of fight'. The dreaded c-word, capitulation, was ready to be used.

Revenge is high on the wishlist of English observers who remember the eight Australian Ashes series wins from 1989-2002. More than another tense summer to match 2005 and 2009, they crave the obliteration of Clarke's team here and again this winter. Total conquest should be England's only aim, they think. They ask: did Waugh or Ponting or Warne or McGrath ever show England any mercy? Did they care about TV viewing figures, newspaper sales or the stretching of dramatic tension across five Tests? No, they sought to wipe out the enemy, to damage him not just for today but for 20 years to come. The scars from that period remain, if the chatter between England fans is any guide. Neutrals and lovers of tight contests want something more.

They want the spirit of Trent Bridge to run right through to the end of August, with England prevailing, of course. When Australia imploded – and fouled up their decision reviews – this series seemed to fall away. An anti-climactic sense settled over Lord's.

Too hasty. Siddle, who took five English first innings wickets at Trent Bridge, reached for his rapier again and cast doubt on England's own batting potency. Pietersen has scored 14, 64, 2 and 5; Cook has hit 13, 50, 12 and 8. Joe Root has yet to establish his authority as an Ashes opener.

England were 31 for three at stumps, a lead of 264. By no stretch could they be said to have fully capitalised on the weakness of Australia's top six, who came into this series with a 70-run per innings disadvantage on average.

Day Three
July 21 Scyld Berry

England (361 & 320-5) lead Australia (128) by 553 runs

A Test match between England and Australia at Lord's is the cricket fixture of all cricket fixtures, as it has been for well over a hundred years.

This has not been the Test of all Tests, however, because England have been so vastly superior to their opponents. Never since the 1880s have England been so far ahead of

Australia in batting as they are now, thanks mainly to Ian Bell and Joe Root, who trashed Australia's bowling as it has never been trashed before at Lord's.

This is the 35th Test match between England and Australia here and only in 1930 have England scored more than 350 in both of their innings, as they will do if they bat on briefly this morning before Alastair Cook's declaration. Back then their totals were nowhere near sufficient, because Don Bradman racked up 254 off his own brilliant bat.

By accelerating after tea and adding 302 runs yesterday to their overnight 31 for three, England doomed Australia to a second defeat and, in effect, retained the Ashes. Neither country has come from behind to win three Tests in a row in England, and the only case in Australia came when Tests were timeless.

This Lord's pitch is far too dry and worn to permit any other outcome than an England victory. At the outset it was 'a day three pitch', and yesterday even Australia's two apprentice spinners made some balls kick and spit out of the rough: Root might add to his enjoyment today as Graeme Swann's fellow off-spinner, even if does not convert his overnight score into a double-century.

Extending an already large lead in the third innings can often be dull fare but Root saved yesterday from being an example, even if England added only 140 in the first two sessions. The Yorkshire batsman had to prove his credentials as an opener worthy to be Cook's partner, and he did so utterly conclusively by seeing off the final fling by Australia's pace bowlers before pummelling their spinners.

Root is 22, only one year older than Bradman when he played what he later called the innings of his life here, and he sealed his place for years to come with his 178 off 334 balls. Except perhaps for the next Test, if Kevin Pietersen's calf strain proves serious: for such is Root's versatility that he could easily slot in as Pietersen's replacement at No 4 and allow Nick Compton to return as opening bat.

Root blunted Australia throughout the morning in company with Tim Bresnan, who was more than a nightwatchman in contributing to a 99-run partnership. With Bell for the fifth wicket Root then added 153 at ever-increasing speed, reducing Michael Clarke to such helplessness that he never bothered to take the second new ball or to flog the knackered horses that his seamers have become through the inadequacies of his batsmen, who never give their team-mates a rest.

Root's shot-selection was disciplined when it had to be, the only question being whether he was too inclined to play back to full-length balls: but this trait is more likely to get him into trouble when the ball is swinging into him, not away as it did yesterday. By the end his shot-selection was unrestrained, and in one over he carted Steve Smith to leg for the second and third sixes of his nascent career.

Bell's innings was notable as much for a poor umpiring decision as for its 74 runs. The decision came when, having scored only three, Bell steered a catch off Ryan Harris very low to gully where Steve Smith dived low to his right and – to most experienced eyes – got his fingers under the ball, before raising his right finger in Bell's direction.

The umpire at the bowler's end, Marais Erasmus, could

have given Bell out and left him to ask for a review if he truly felt aggrieved. Instead, the on-field umpires consulted with their colleague Tony Hill, who interpreted the television pictures as a not-out. Hill, 62, does not have any significant playing experience to call on.

The question for Australia in the rest of this series is which timbers are sound enough to be used to build their future. Usman Khawaja does not look to be one of them. Like Graeme Hick or Mark Ramprakash, he is in and out of the side, up and down the order, and given every chance to fail.

So much Australian time and faith have been invested in Phil Hughes that he may be given the whole of this series to justify them. David Warner, however, will surely replace Khawaja for the third Test in Manchester, whatever he does in southern Africa during his rehabilitation.

James Pattinson improved markedly in the course of England's second innings and bowled 18 overs for only 24 runs before he was switched to the pavilion end – a costly experiment. But he had performed like a Test-class seam-and-swing bowler until then.

By his expensive first-innings bowling, he also illustrated why the Australians have been so unsuccessful at Lord's since 2005, and so successful before then. Now they are given no trial run with the slope before the Test, but in former years they would be given a practice game against Middlesex or MCC; and perhaps at Canterbury too, the closest simulation to the Lord's slope.

Ashton Agar initially did the job of holding the line for Australia, giving Clarke some control by bowling his first 13 overs for 25 runs. True, Agar had to bowl increasingly over the wicket and into the rough to be so economical, but at least he allowed the footsore seamers some respite.

When Root and Bell accelerated, however, his youthfulness was exposed and he was driven through the covers. Steadiness and over-spin are not enough. He will have to make significant runs in Australia's second innings to retain his place ahead of the off-spinner Nathan Lyon, who at least takes his share of wickets.

Australia's wheels have not come off, yet, but England's work this winter will be so much easier if they do. The last time they fell off on a tour of England was in 1985, when again Australia had only one top-class batsman, Allan Border.

Cunningly, England's senior players then detached Border from the rest of his team by making him an honorary Englishman: come along and play golf with us, AB, you're one of us, forget those losers. Clarke has shown individualistic tendencies, before he was captain, and Australia will go into freefall if he should become detached.

July 21 Steve James

Humiliation is best prepared slowly and surely, and England did not need to rush the rubbing of Australian noses in the dirt.

The pitch, deliberately drier than usual at England's behest, may have been hampering strokeplay with its stickiness and increasing unevenness, but the truth is that this was a day for England to inflict the utmost pain, however long it took. Only at the end was the heat turned up. They do not do frippery in such situations, for which they are often accused of excessive conservatism. But pragmatism can rest easily in Test cricket.

And anyway when a young man like Joe Root is scoring his first Ashes century, his first as a Test opener, then he can take as long as he desires.

As long as he has learnt (and he does learn remarkably quickly) that the straight-batted back-foot force (from which he should have been dismissed on Friday night) is fraught with danger against the new ball, then a quite glorious career awaits at the top of the order.

It may just be that this was the day on which England finally settled themselves away from the baffling freneticism that has characterised too much of the play in this series, and also the day on which the Australians realised that there is simply no way back this summer.

Yes, it was the fault of the visiting batsmen's abject collapse on Friday, but it was the bowlers who were suffering now. And both departments could be scarred for the series. For instance, the longer the heavy-boned Ryan Harris was in the field, the shorter, you sensed, his series would be.

It could be argued that the edge had gone out of the contest by Saturday morning with England already 264 runs ahead, but they had, after all, lost three swift wickets the previous evening, so I think this presented some of the series' best cricket here. It had a control and class so often lacking before. By the end Root was simply magisterial.

Heresy it might be to say as much, but for all the frills,

spills, drama and hype so far in this series, there has also been some distinctly poor-quality cricket played. And not all of it by Australia.

For all the excellence of James Anderson, Ian Bell, Root yesterday and the wickets of Graeme Swann without bowling particularly well, England have also delved quite regularly into the lockers marked mediocrity.

Alastair Cook (head falling over), Jonathan Trott (what an odd shot here) and Kevin Pietersen (rusty and calf-strung) are all struggling with the bat. Jonny Bairstow, for all his run-gathering nous, has a technical worry. Steven Finn bowled very poorly at Trent Bridge. And Stuart Broad's hot and cold phases have not reached the steaming stage yet, at least with the ball.

So the top-rankers South Africa will not have been quaking in their boots (not that England play them soon – not until the winter of 2015-16 in fact), and the improving India, who come here for five Tests next summer, might just be eyeing events with quiet confidence. But at least England possess mainly proven Test cricketers. They will doubtless improve. Australia? Trent Bridge might just have been their apex.

Even still they made a very un-Australian selection in dropping Ed Cowan after just one Test. Cowan reckoned he had 'kept his head above water' during the recent 4-0 thrashing in India. But he had no luck in the series build-up – receiving two shocking decisions at Taunton and Worcester, getting hit on the head at short leg and falling ill at Trent Bridge – and still the selectors pushed him under last week.

Michael Clarke's reign is being defined by a revolving-door

selection policy. It is aping England's worst times, which is a change, because since losing the last Ashes Down Under in 2010-11, Australia, acting upon the Argus report, have generally been trying to ape England's best times of late. But, as the sacking of Mickey Arthur proved, it is just not working. Each country must play to its strengths. England tried to copy Australia for too long. We looked for non-existent leg-spinners and idolised their state cricket. Now we are working around our own system. Even our biggest Australianism – a national academy – is different in that, at Loughborough, it is set apart from the traditional cricket centres, whereas Australia's, once in Adelaide, is now in Brisbane and linked in with Queensland cricket.

England cricketers are being polished in Loughborough. That is clearly not so in Brisbane, certainly not batsmen anyway.

July 21 Paul Hayward

Joe Root is not a reader. He says he once made it 'halfway' through John Grisham's The Client. But his Test career should run to many volumes. Line-by-line patience was a virtue of his maiden Ashes century here at Lord's: the first by a Yorkshireman against Australia in front of the Long Room since Len Hutton and Willie Watson in the same match in 1953.

With arms aloft, and laddish features glowing, Root also became the youngest batsman to make an Ashes century for England at Lord's at 22 years and 202 days. Applauding him from the Pavillion were a weekend cast of men in egg and bacon blazers and Panamas. Down the years they will have cheered many flinty Yorkshiremen, but few who send out tweets about 'Northern Monkey Clothing' and Nando's, or take photographs of boxes of Yorkshire Tea.

Yes: Root has been delivered to English Test cricket via a marketing director's dream. He is a northern bridge to the next generation. His is the world of cheery mass communication. His face radiates youth and optimism. But it would all be hollow without the batting, without the runs.

His elevation to the England starting XI has now been fully justified. In a Test series of low scores for openers he has shown more experienced colleagues how to construct an innings of winning quality. A major star is born.

Australia landed the first punch on him, but the knockout goes to him. The jab thrown by David Warner in a bar in Birmingham has now been avenged out on the pitch. Warner, the disgraced Australian batsman, might wish he had landed more cleanly. The glancing blow sustained by Root did nothing to deter him or stifle his boyish vigour.

This was his second century in three Tests. The first came on home turf at Headingley, against New Zealand. For a 22-year-old to wow the Independent Republic of Yorkshire and the Establishment here at Lord's in one summer is quite a feat. To people from other counties, the Yorkshire angle must be baffling. What is it about the land of blunt speaking that earns it special treatment in the recording of statistics? In the national context, is Root's Yorkshire-ness really important at all?

We might as well say yes, if only to avoid the letters from Leeds and Halifax. Plainly, Root represents a local tradition, as does his brother, Billy, who is on the 12th-man staff for this Test, and who gave his sibling a real good hug after carrying out the drinks. One for the family album.

There is a lot to like about the pair, as well as Yorkshire's talent production line. With Root on national service, his county place against Derbyshire was taken by Alex Lees, 20, who struck 275 not out. Geoffrey Boycott has waxed about Lees for a couple of years, and we could yet see him and Root leading the way for England three or four years from now. Not forgetting Tim Bresnan or Jonny Bairstow, England's No 6, from Bradford, who joined his younger county colleague at the crease at 282 for five.

With his century filed away, Root cut loose, smashing two sixes off Steve Smith in the penultimate over to finish unbeaten on 178. Promoted to opener at Nick Compton's expense, he is a fine advertisement for the English player development system. He played at every representative level on the climb to this day at Lord's, which came seven months after his debut in Nagpur, where he scored 73 from 229 balls at No 6 against India.

'I'd never heard of him', Kevin Pietersen said in an interview this summer. 'He walked out and just his face walking towards me for 20 metres – I thought, this kid's going to be a flipping superstar. It was just the confidence that he walked out to bat with in his debut Test match in India, two spinners bowling, from each end.

'He walked out with a smile on his face, and went: 'Alright

lad, you OK, you're batting well there'. And I was like – mate, I've played 90-odd Tests and I don't walk out like that. But it's brilliant for English cricket. Absolutely brilliant.'

'One minute you're watching these boys on the telly, and all of a sudden I'm in the dressing room and going out for dinner with them,' Root said after that encouraging bow.

The Warner incident, in which Root is said to have been wearing a green and gold wig on his chin, might have upset his equilibrium, or earned him a reputation as a larrikin, but it soon passed into the trivia bin. 'What impressed me was that he was under intense scrutiny for a couple of days but he still went out and played against Sri Lanka [in the Champions Trophy], even though we lost the game, and got 70-odd at nearly a run a ball,' said Alastair Cook, the England captain. 'That showed me he could handle the pressure.' After Root passed 1,000 first-class runs for the season, he glided past 150 in this innings and looked like he might never leave the crease.

And as if to prove his youth (some MCC members may not follow this), his nickname in the dressing room is 'Wireless', as in, wireless router (geddit?) Confirmation of his talent will buzz by router all around the cricket world.

July 21 Shane Warne

This match is now a test of character for Australia's batsmen. There are some very talented guys in the Australian team with an opportunity for a long career in front of them.

Cricket is a performance-based game and crikey, the time to perform is right now.

It is still a good pitch. Yes, it will turn, yes there will be reverse swing in the second innings but it is not a minefield. Australia should back themselves to still draw the game and stay in the series. They cannot afford to lose at Lord's and go down 2-0. Winning the three remaining matches to regain the Ashes would be an incredibly tough task.

All the batsmen have got in at some point in the series. The puzzle is why they are not making significant scores. Firstly, credit has to go to England and their bowlers but if you look at the dismissals at Lord's only Steven Smith was actually bowled out by a good delivery. The rest were architects of their own downfall. Phil Hughes thought he was Brian Lara trying to drive expansively at a wide ball before he got in, Chris Rogers was out to the worst ball I have seen in Test cricket that got a wicket and Usman Khawaja had a brain fade.

In fact he could have been out three times before he reached double figures. The Australian batsmen are playing adrenalin cricket and are in a hurry to impose themselves on England. Patience is the key. They have to trust their defence and bat for long periods of time without going into their shell.

In Test cricket it is about finding the right balance. It comes from batting with confidence. It is about summing up the situation of the game. What is required now for the team? They need to build partnerships by rotating the strike, hitting the bad balls and make the bowlers bowl to them. I know it is basic stuff but when things are not going right you sometimes forget the basics.

Once again Australia messed up the review system. It is your wild card and a vital part of the modern game. They wasted one (Shane Watson) and then did not use it when the umpire had made a mistake (Rogers). Without those errors Australia would not have been bowled out for 128. That shows how important the DRS has become.

I believe Watson is batting in the right position. We know he is a class act but many people are frustrated with his failure to make the big score. He wants to dominate the bowlers, which he can. To me it looks as though his mindset is, 'I've seen off James Anderson, now it's time to impose myself on this England attack'. One of the basics you are taught as a 10- year-old is to play in the 'V' at the start of your innings. That simple basic still holds true for him now.

His problem is not technical. It is mental. In 1989 Graham Gooch had lots of throw downs to try and make himself play straight but as soon as he got out in the middle, he played across the line and Terry Alderman had him lbw. Sometimes a weakness becomes an addiction. With such an inexperienced side, Australia need Watson making runs at the top of the order.

Australia have to be strong and resist tinkering with the batting order too much. When you lose, you search for the right combination that would suddenly make everything click. It is easy to over-complicate and think too hard. You have to say 'this is the batting order. Go out and make the runs'. The fewer the changes, the better.

Michael Clarke has shifted down to No 5. If that is where he makes the most runs for Australia then it has to be the right decision for the team. But once that call has been made, stick with it. Clarke has to find a way to clear his mind. The Mickey Arthur controversy before the match and the stuff about an alleged bad relationship with Watson, which is rubbish by the way, swirling around him before the Test. It is not easy as captain to then go out and make the runs your team requires.

There are not too many options for Australia. David Warner will be back in time for the third Test but will not have played any cricket in England since the Champions Trophy match in June.

They would like to get James Faulkner in the side but that would mean dropping one of the bowlers, which would be very harsh. They have shown character and skill to put Australia into good positions.

Clarke knows he has an attack that will take 20 wickets. The problems lie elsewhere. The bowlers have done a great job for Australia with barely any rest. And Australia have to be careful a culture of 'we've done our job, why don't you do yours?' does not build up between the bowlers and batsmen.

July 21 Simon Hughes

This is shaping into an annus mirabilis for Joe Root. The England selectors made a big call when they plumped for him to open the batting in the Ashes. Nick Compton was the man in possession and had certainly not let England down, with two determined centuries in New Zealand and some other painstaking efforts. But selectors are paid to have hunches and they could see the unravelling of one man and the unveiling of another. He repaid that decision with a special innings yesterday. There were few moments when you doubted that he would become the first Yorkshireman to make a hundred at Lord's against Australia since our own Geoff Boycott in 1980.

The crucial evidence to encourage Root's promotion was supplied at Headingley in the test against New Zealand. Compton looked tense and heavy-footed and his technique appeared to have a major flaw. Shackled with an intense desire to succeed, he planted his foot on leg stump and played everything from that position which made him vulnerable to the ball nipping back from off stump (he was bowled through the gate at Lord's) and the wider one moving away (he was caught at slip in the first innings at Headingley.)

Root had already compiled a sublime hundred in England's first innings at Leeds – batting at No 5 – and when Compton struggled to seven in an hour and a half in England's second innings before being caught at short leg off the part-time spin of Kane Williamson, the selectors' minds were made up.

What influenced their decision as much as Root's method was his mindset. He seemed calm and unflustered at the crease, but busy too, always on the lookout for singles, there was security and yet good purpose in his batting. He had an excellent awareness of what the bowlers were trying to do and the match situation. It had been a demonstration of smart batting.

We were treated to six hours of that by Root yesterday. The Australians gave him a helping hand with a pleasant leg stump half volley first ball of the morning from Peter Siddle. Clinically, Root put it away wide of mid-on. Afterwards the bowlers were more disciplined, and made Root earn his runs.

He was neat and compact in defence, playing the ball almost daringly late, right under his nose. This is a significant contrast to Compton who tends to commit to the front foot and go searching for the ball more. He is a rather rigid player where Root glides about the crease, shifting generally onto the backfoot, riding the ball's movement, sometimes a little slow to get forward when the ball is full but careful not to be drawn into playing away from his body.

He has the face of a choirboy but the worldliness of a minister. There is superb organisation and control in his play. The defence is secure, the judgment of what to leave and what to play almost flawless, but he is an opportunist, always looking to score. There were cuffs backward of square if the ball was short, firm pushes through mid-wicket, deft glances and nifty dabs. Calls to his partner are clear and immediate. One square drive, played with body leaning well forward, back foot low to the ground, was an all-time classic, the ball laser-guided to the boundary into the gap square of the wicket.

Despite his youth, he doesn't expend excess energy at the crease, strolling casually to square leg between balls, smiling contentedly, clearly relishing the contest. He rehearses shots after the delivery, but not in an anxious, concerned way, more just to groove his movements. It was like a master craftsman polishing his tools. It was hard to believe this was not his 80th Test, but his eighth.

When he got into the forties he registered his 1000th first class run of the summer – average 90 – and soon after steered a ball, Michael Atherton-like, through backward point to bring up his first Ashes fifty. A straight drive just before lunch had the essence of Michael Vaughan. After weathering a brief run drought in the 70s, as the Australians at last managed to string a few decent deliveries together, he progressed to 99, and, betraying no nerves, made room to square cut Ashton Agar and go to three figures. He had attained what neither Vaughan nor Atherton had managed – making an Ashes century at the Mecca of cricket.

It was a wretched day for Australia, starting with a leg stump gimme and rarely improving. It took them until 45 minutes after lunch to prise out the nightwatchman Tim Bresnan, and saw a reputable catch denied them by the limitations of the TV cameras. Facing their sixth successive Test defeat, this is rapidly becoming their *annus horribilis*.

Day Four
July 22 Derek Pringle

England (361 & 349-7) beat Australia (128 & 235) by 347 runs

It was the obituary of English cricket in 1882 that led to the creation of the Ashes but Australia are trying to create a fresh corpse for cremation after they fell to their fourth Ashes defeat in a row at Lord's yesterday.

The final rites, at least for this match, were administered by Graeme Swann with three balls of the day's play left. Amid lengthening shadows and a packed Mound Stand bathed in golden evening light, Swann, who finished with match figures of nine for 122, turned one down the slope to have James Pattinson lbw, Australia's humiliation complete in their inability to take the game into a final day. No wonder their captain admitted they are a virtual laughing stock.

The defeat, by 347 runs with a day and three balls of the match remaining, leaves Australia and the series, as a contest at least, in a parlous state. To prevent England retaining the urn for a third successive time, they need to boldly go where no team has gone before since Tests ceased to be timeless, and come back from 2-0 down to win the last three matches.

They will take some resurrecting. This was England's biggest defeat of them at home in terms of runs, eclipsing the 289-run win at the Oval in 1926. That match was the first of five Ashes wins in succession, the last of them in 1929, the only occasion other than yesterday England had won four in a row. That heady run in the 1920s coincided with the start of Sir Donald Bradman's career but there is nobody starting out in this Australian side, other than Pattinson, who looks like they could be the next big thing.

This was Australia's sixth successive defeat in Tests, a sequence of woe last experienced 29 years ago when they were flogged by the West Indies, indisputably the best team in the world at the time. This England team are not in that league, but they outclassed Michael Clarke's team in all departments.

For the second time in the match, and the third time in the series, Australia's batsmen failed to show more than a passing desire for occupation of the crease. Usman Khawaja and Clarke both made fifties but just as a mini renaissance threatened to dispense a drip of comfort throughout the dressing room, both got out in soft ways to the spin of Joe Root.

England have not produced flawless cricket here at Lord's but unlike the previous match at Trent Bridge, there they had to engage their reserve tank, they only needed to find overdrive on a few occasions, the most obvious being Root's 180 in the second innings and Ian Bell's 109 in the first. Otherwise their batting and bowling has been no more than beta plus, but then it has not needed to be, so poor is Australia's morale at present.

When play began yesterday, England batted on, presumably to allow Root the chance of a double hundred. He missed the milestone though, England adding just 16 runs before he was caught at third man off Harris for 180 playing a scoop shot. With a nominal 583 to make, Australia faced the prospect of surviving 170 overs, a task Shane Watson approached with a lunging left foot and a hefty swing of the bat. Stuart Broad was smashed over the top of mid-off for four then cut to the third man rope.

Like so many batsmen with a signature shot, his being the booming drive, it can be a weakness too and when he planted his front foot on off-stump to Anderson he was lbw when the ball nipped back down the slope. He did not invoke the Decision Review System, much to the relief of team mates, as he would have wasted a review. Not that they were used wisely and after Swann had bowled Rogers, following a complete misjudgement from the left-hander who offered no stroke as the ball crashed into his off stump, Phillip Hughes asked to review an lbw that was always hitting the stumps.

Khawaja and Clarke then added 98 in a stand that mixed attack with defence though Clarke should have been stumped by Matt Prior when he was on two, following one of his sorties down the pitch to Swann. Khawaja did not try to delay England with bat alone, his collision with Swann, as he scampered to make his ground following a quick single, knocked Swann over, hurting his back. The discomfort was enough for him to vacate his perch at second slip and for Cook to bring Root on in his place. But Root can bowl a bit and he had Clarke caught at leg slip and Khawaja caught in the gully off successive overs.

Steve Smith used up the last review when Tim Bresnan found his inside-edge, though Hot Spot failed to spark at least on the non-high-definition monitors in the media centre. It did not light up either when England reviewed Ashton Agar's swish at Bresnan soon after, but that did not stop TV umpire Tony Hill overruling Marais Erasmus's original not out decision on sound from the stump microphones.

Brad Haddin fell to Swann and Peter Siddle to Anderson before another 10th-wicket stand between Pattinson and Ryan Harris held up England long enough for them to take the second new ball and the extra half hour. But with that almost up too, Swann struck to clinch the victory.

When England's cricket teams were routinely getting skewered in the Ashes between 1989 and 2005, mischievous Aussie administrators used to suggest playing England over four-day Tests. Well this one finished just inside that limit, so perhaps it should be put back on the table, with the hope it might bring them an odd draw, at least until they find their feet again.

July 22 Geoffrey Boycott

If you cannot bat, you cannot win. Until Australia solve their batting problems they have not a cat in hell's chance of making a game of it against England, never mind winning the Ashes.

Michael Clarke can talk a good game. The coach, Darren Lehmann, can suggest it will improve. The occasional Australian batsman can play a little cameo but that is totally useless until they occupy the crease, show better technique, patience and improve their shot selection.

Even if they win the toss and bat on a very flat pitch they do not have enough ability or mental resolve to stop the England team. They are going to get steamrollered in the same way Australia used to wallop us. Now the boot is on the other foot.

I always thought their batting was a problem but I never dreamt it would be this bad. Without runs you are never in the game and at times the Australian technique or mental application is no better than Zimbabwe or Bangladesh. It is a mismatch.

Shane Watson is a very talented cricketer but at his age it is a bit late to try to alter the way you play. In 79 innings he has got out 31 per cent of the time lbw. He unfurls some really good shots but plays across the line time and time again. There has been no improvement, no change in the way he plays and that is stupid.

Chris Rogers was brought in at the last moment from playing county cricket for Middlesex. He is a stop-gap opener who is not good enough but tries like hell. I commend his defensive efforts to let the ball come to him. He tries to stay in but has not got enough batting ability. You cannot put there what God did not give you.

Usman Khawaja looks a decent player. He just made a mental error in the first innings by stupidly trying to hit Graeme Swann over the top. In the second innings he learnt his lesson, knuckled down and played really well. He got forward to the turning ball smothering the spin, he had the patience to wait for Swann to bowl too straight and worked him on the on side either off the front foot or pulling him. Seamers were not a problem to him. Anything slightly short, he put away with an excellent pull shot. What he needs to do is go on from here and play the same way again.

Michael Clarke is the one high-quality player. But so far this series he has not done enough for Australia. He got one magic ball at Trent Bridge, played very well here and is one of the world's best. But he is batting with people not in the same class as him.

Phillip Hughes amazed me with an excellent 81 not out at Trent Bridge. He watched the ball carefully on to the bat, tightened up his technique from when he played here four years ago but at Lord's he looked out of his depth. Maybe Trent Bridge was a one-off innings.

Steve Smith looks to me like a player who wants to be aggressive every innings he plays and sometimes it will come off. But he did not seem able to adapt to the situation in the first innings when the ball was turning. He played miles too far in front of his pad, it bounced and he popped it to short leg. In the second innings he played an expansive drive without any foot movement with a stiff left leg. He was miles away from the pitch of the ball. These are elementary mistakes.

The top six in any team has to bat collectively and make the bulk of the team's runs. You cannot leave it to wicket-keepers and tailenders to lift you out of the mire every time. In fact on Sunday if you were a neutral watching the Australian batsmen and then some of the tailenders bat, you would think the tailenders were better players. Peter Siddle, James Pattinson and Ryan Harris looked more comfortable at the crease. That is ridiculous.

Are we English enjoying it? You bet we are. When Australia were thrashing us they lauded it over us, they were so conceited and bombastic, overbearing and up their own backsides that some of their players trashed England. Guys such as Rod Marsh rubbished us to the point of calling our bowlers 'pie chuckers'. There was some truth in it because we were a shambles but this Australian batting line-up is worse than ours used to be.

In 1994-95 we went Down Under and were insulted when they made our national team play a one-day series against Australia and Australia A. Well now I think our England Lions could beat this lot, or at least give them a run for their money. In some ways many of us England supporters want to see Australia thrashed 5-0 and then go to Australia this winter and beat them 5-0 in their own country. In another way it is not good for cricket with such a traditional contest being so one-sided. It was not interesting when they were beating us and it is not so good now. I cannot see them batting much better because it is a bit late to be sorting out your technique in the middle of a Test series. Anybody who put their money on England winning 10-0, which looked fanciful at the time, could be laughing all the way to the bank.

July 22 Scyld Berry

Australia's cricketers departed from Lord's in 2005 in much the same frame of mind as England's supporters on Sunday. The Ashes were in the urn, and the urn was in the bag.

It only took one ball – one stray ball on the Edgbaston outfield, upon which Glenn McGrath trod – to undermine Australia's campaign of eight years ago. That is not to say that England will lose this series from 2-0 up, but that cricket hates hubris and the pendulum can suddenly swing.

The margin of victory – England's second largest over Australia in terms of runs – should not be allowed to conceal the fact that England in both innings lost their first three wickets before reaching 30. To the rescue came Ian Bell and Joe Root, but such poor starts are overcome so seldom that only twice before had England won a Test from this position.

Any Test team that can cut through their opponents' top order as Australia did at least has the basic requirement of penetrative pace bowling. What Michael Clarke and Darren Lehmann have to do is make the most of their remaining resources, not in the hope of winning this series but to build a credible side for the return series in Australia.

England supporters predicting 5-0 this summer could bear in mind that Australia's Plan A has yet to fail. David Warner should have been opening the batting with Shane Watson, and can be expected to do so in the third Test at Old Trafford. It may not be a partnership that lasts for long periods, but it will have considerable impact while it does.

Chris Rogers has to cure his tendency to look guilty when England appeal for lbw: he looks at the umpire, which invites him to raise his finger, then jumps back into position as if the rabbit-proof fence in Western Australia was designed to keep him out. But his first-class record suggests he can bat all day, like Root on Saturday or the matured Bell, and if he can do so Australia will become a competitive side.

Usman Khawaja's calm half-century was oil on Australia's troubled waters and should have secured him a longer run than the normal three or four Tests he has been given before being dropped. However, his limited footwork and penchant for square-of-the-wicket strokes suggest he would be more suited to No 4, behind Rogers.

Much time and faith has been invested in Phil Hughes, and he did contribute 81 not out at No 6 in the first Test to Australia's last-wicket stand of 163, but without ever looking as authoritative as Ashton Agar. Graeme Swann in particular is now tormenting Hughes, who has his twin strengths of cut and cover-drive, and so little else besides.

Hughes looks lopsided by comparison with Nic Maddinson, another left-hander from New South Wales, but younger at 22 and a strokemaker all round the wicket. Maddinson featured only on Australia's A tour of England but when he scored 181 against Gloucestershire and batted alongside Hughes, one looked a Test batsman in the making and the other did not.

Steve Smith may not be a Test-class batsman either, to judge by his wildness yesterday when he lapsed into his old habit of driving with a stiff front leg. But Australia will have to pick either him or Hughes or Ed Cowan for the rest of this series, and Smith's leg-break – when it lands – will be worth having at Old Trafford, which is likely to take even more spin than the other over-dry pitches of this series.

Promising as Agar's batting is, he has taken only two wickets in his main role and has to be replaced by Nathan Lyon. While England have Swann and Root to aim into the footmarks created by the pace bowlers of both sides, Australia have been artless in having no off-spinner of their own.

Smith is like so many England players of the 1990s: promoted to the Test side on the strength of being a decent bits-and-pieces cricketer in limited-overs formats. Australia's administrators are powerless to do anything about the Indian Premier League and the big money for T20 players, but they are culpable for having destroyed their traditional strengths and saturating their calendar with limited-overs quantity.

They reduced the importance of the Sheffield Shield by renaming it the Pura Milk Cup. They introduced a convoluted one-day competition in which a state bats for 45 overs divided into two innings, and which again distracts batsmen from building an innings. Clarke and Lehmann have been left to assemble a ship from this wreckage, and no wonder it sinks.

July 22 Paul Hayward

Cricket Germany has offered to replace England as Australia's opponents.

'If you fancy a competitive game we are only an hour's flight from London,' tweeted the Deutscher Cricket Bund, thus proving that Germans have a sense of humour after all and that Australia have exposed themselves to ridicule.

Over-fed with drama for the past year, we thought this Ashes series would ignite another glorious summer. Trent Bridge tricked us. Lord's told the truth. However much the English want a 5-0 victory they would prefer a contest first.

Germany's offer cannot be taken up. Technically the urn is still up for grabs. All Australia need to do to turn this series round is to win the Tests in Manchester, Durham and at the Oval with a group of batsman who were 117 for nine at one stage at Trent Bridge and were removed for 128 and 235 at Lord's. They are surviving on 10th-wicket stands. All England need is a draw from those three fixtures to keep the little pot of dust.

The two Tests so far have not lacked talking points, romance, controversy or classic Ashes snapshots, such as Ashton Agar's 98 in Nottingham and Joe Root's 180 and two major wickets here. The Decision Review System has kept us supplied with courtroom capers and Australia have appeared confused by all forms of technology, including the older kind, of bat and ball.

On the day of their impaling at the game's spiritual home, Cricket Australia was forced to issue a statement on behalf of David Warner – himself already in the doghouse – disassociating him from a rude tweet sent by his brother about Shane Watson, the opening batsman who extended his collection of false dawns by falling lbw to James Anderson for 20.

On the averages, and Australia's recent Test record, England's superiority here is no great surprise. At Trent Bridge, Darren Lehmann's team overachieved, creeping to within 14 runs of a famous victory after needing 80 to win with nine wickets down. It was always hard to imagine them improving much on that performance. England, on the other hand, were bound to come on for the run. But nobody could have expected such a graphic illustration of Australian weaknesses, or for the series to expire so fast.

The magical aura of a Lord's Ashes Test was certainly detectable when Australia flew in their legends to inspire by example. And the steady flow of politicians, musicians, actors and other celebrities into the Test Match Special commentary box was testament to the excitement generated in Nottingham. Both David Cameron and Ed Miliband paraded their love of cricket. Across the whole social scene it was clearly hip to be seen at Lord's. In England, after a year of prizes and bunting, sport is almost guaranteed to confer good days out.

Few came to Lord's expecting a massacre. In most minds still were the long tussles of 2005 and 2009. Australia might not be much to look at but they had a new coach and a bit more bite. The long hot summer was unfolding nicely. England's first innings brought another century for Ian Bell but no suggestion of a mismatch, even if England had been 28 for three before amassing 361.

On this batting pitch, Australia could expect a big score of their own. But then Watson fell to the last ball before lunch and wasted a review. Watson's selfishness in placing his own vain hope before the needs of his team seemed to detonate the Australian innings spiritually. Chris Rogers, Usman Khawaja, Michael Clarke and Steve Smith all went cheaply as they collapsed to 128 all out.

There are days in Tests when teams are dismantled and destroyed before your eyes. It feels terminal, but seldom is. Over the long narrative of a series recoveries are possible, even likely. Yet not one of the great Australians working in the media here made a case for a revival. None said the batting would improve. Not a soul stepped up to argue that personnel changes could save this team. Nathan Lyon for Agar, who made no impact with the ball, is one obvious alteration. There is, though, no phalanx of talented replacements, unless one counts the recently discarded or retired: Simon Katich, Phil Jacques, Michael Hussey or even Ricky Ponting.

England have not needed to be especially good to reach this dominant position. Good in places, but not great across the board. These Tests have allowed them to write Root's name on the Long Room board, to augment Bell's new status as a middle-order saviour and to bring their bowlers up to a higher grade of accuracy than they were able to reach in Nottingham.

Australia, on the other hand, look bereft, not just now but for years to come. They are hounded by questions. Why has the talent production line broken down? Where is their Joe Root? Is Twenty20 destroying Australian technique? Are they the new West Indies?

Acceptance, resignation, hangs over this side. Few expect that mood to lift much this side of back-to-back series. English complacency could restore the spark to this one. Australia's internal tensions could ease. The abuse they will 'cop' back home could yet tap into some deep well of pride and defiance and bring them snarling to Old Trafford. But there is no celestial hand that can reach down and make this side better than they really are. It cannot sprinkle extra ability on Clarke's team, who endured their second biggest defeat to England by margin of runs (347). England were not remotely pressurised in this Test, which is a shame for them too. They need a competitive series to help them develop.

The year that keeps on giving has decided to be less liberal with its gifts. One-sidedness has replaced gnawing tension. Only England's margin of victory in this series appears in doubt. At least now we know we can always call the Germans in and call it Der Ashes.

July 22 Simon Hughes

Jimmy Anderson is tormenting Shane Watson as Glenn McGrath used to torture Michael Atherton. Nineteen times the towering McGrath saw off England's opening batsman and linchpin, and you could see concern in his features every time Atherton took guard to Australia's irrepressible fast bowler. At the top of a fragile batting order, he knew that through him lay the gateway to victory.

Anderson is having the same effect on Watson. Not necessarily in the number of dismissals, though he trapped him lbw on Sunday after Watson's customary purposeful start, but in the way he is messing with his technique and resolve. Watson was deliberately reinstalled at the top of the Australian order to do a job on Anderson, to try and take England's spearhead down a peg or two.

The opposite seems to have happened. Watson, a hugely talented batsman, who habitually destroys bowling attacks in the shorter form of the game, wears a haunted look when he faces Anderson. He still unfurls a few meaty drives, but there is a lack of permanence about him, as you might expect from a man who has been out 27 times (in 79 innings) between 20 and 49 and consequently averages 35 in Test cricket. He bats as if he expects the unplayable ball or the umpire's raised finger at any time. His self-belief appears to have a finite time span.

Anderson and his colleagues have hassled and harassed Watson so consistently he finally felt obliged to change his technique. He has been out lbw once every three Test innings and having been dismissed that way in his last two knocks in this series, it had finally got to him. He was beginning to accept that his strength is his weakness. The fact that he plants his front foot down the wicket allows him to play his booming drives to balls that others would defend. But it is also a rigid position, which he cannot adjust if the ball moves and threatens his pads.

So on Sunday he took guard further outside leg stump, making sure he kept his leg out of the way and could get his bat to the ball. It worked temporarily. He bunted a couple of strong drives down the ground and squirted one through cover. Anderson swung a couple away and they were thick edged into the slips. Watson needed all his expertise to keep the fast bowler out.

A sensitive soul, what was also playing on Watson's mind was the previous misuse of the DRS. It has caused quite a furore around the team, with him rather unfairly portrayed as the main culprit. The Australian media are unforgiving and David Warner's brother accused him on Twitter of being selfish for using up a review when he was palpably out. In fact his employment of the review is more a case of him being in denial, unable to accept that he had missed another straight ball having done the initial due diligence and got into the thirties.

Anderson, a forensic examiner of technique in the way that McGrath was, is not a man to face when your focus is corrupted. Such is his control he was bowling to an extraordinary field – no one at long leg or deep square, a man at deep midwicket, a wide mid-on and a catcher standing almost in front of the non-striker. Everyone else was on the off side. His intentions were clear. He was going to keep the ball pitched up on off stump and look for a little bit of movement either way.

The prospect of a ball nipping back down the slope and rapping Watson on the pad was as inevitable as exorbitant boutiques in St John's Wood High Street. When the moment came, there was a time lapse before Marais Erasmus gave him out almost as if he did not have the heart to do it. Would Watson review it? Though there was a remote possibility that the ball had hit the bat first, Watson knew he could not afford to waste another one, so, with an expression of weary resignation, went on his way.

Watson encapsulates Australia's problem. They have talent. But, against a superior team in conditions made to suit them, they ultimately expect to fail. And once that feeling percolates the subconscious you are dead.

Third Test Old Trafford Day One
August 2 Derek Pringle

Australia (303-3) v England

Michael Clarke has split Australia with his quirky captaincy but he would have united the country with a Test hundred that was both classical in nature and crucial in its timing.

Since going 2-0 down at Lord's, Clarke has repeatedly peddled the optimistic line that Australia can still win the Ashes, so both he and the team needed a score if that notion were ever to be taken remotely seriously.

Yesterday, in front of a sell-out crowd at the new Old Trafford, he delivered in the third Investec Test a captain's innings to give him and his team some wriggle room as they closed on 303 for three to head a Test match for the first time in the series.

The century was his 24th in Tests, but while it was not his most sparkling, it had restorative powers, lifting team members such as Steve Smith who, like a lucky charm, kept his master company as England's bowlers huffed and puffed on the most stroke-friendly pitch of the series. The pair had added 174 runs by the close, their first 100-plus partnership by batsmen from the top six.

Prior to yesterday's hundred, Clarke had looked ill at

ease with his batting against England. Their plan, hatched in Australia three years ago, was to bowl at an imaginary fifth stump and let Clarke's impatience and technical flaw of playing away from his body with a diagonal bat prove his undoing. They strayed from that plan yesterday, not by much, but enough for him to get a brisk start and feel more secure at the crease than of late.

Clarke's bad back has often hampered him as well, but a muggy Manchester day would have freed that, while the do-or-die state of the series would have done the same for his mind. He also won his first toss of the series, though the advantages of that could be marginal unless the pitch breaks up by day three.

Knowing that you have to deliver can liberate as many as it limits, and Clarke followed Chris Rogers' lead by putting away the loose balls at the start of his innings. That early acuity as well as England's inaccuracy could be seen in the figures, Clarke's first fifty taking 67 balls, his second, as England bowlers tightened their discipline, 102 balls.

Rogers, who had admitted earlier in the week that he had been trying too hard, gave Australia the start they had lacked since the second innings at Trent Bridge, when Shane Watson did most of the running.

In the gap between this Test and Lord's both men stayed in London to work on their games. But while Rogers worked at being more relaxed at the crease, Watson looked tenser than normal, pushing stiffly enough at a ball from Tim Bresnan for the catch to fly to Alastair Cook at first slip.

The grip in the match affected England too, with James

Anderson also falling into the trap of trying too hard. Before play, a grateful Lancashire presented him with a silver salver for becoming the county's greatest wicket-taker for England in Tests with 318, a tally he had not advanced in the 21 overs he had bowled by the close.

Just before tea, Anderson was convinced he had Smith caught behind when the batsman was on 18, just as Graeme Swann felt he had him lbw when he was on nought. On both occasions Smith was given not out, and while both were reviewed by England, both the original decisions were upheld by the TV umpire.

If both conclusions were understandable, in the absence of strong contrary evidence, England were made vulnerable for having used up their quota of reviews.

With the umpiring never less than nervy, it was a situation that was always likely to cost them and when Stuart Broad thudded an inswinger into Smith's pads soon after tea, umpire Tony Hill declined to see what Hawk-Eye had, which was the ball hitting middle stump three quarters of the way up.

If England felt aggrieved, and Broad has now spent 45 overs on 199 Test wickets, they had benefited earlier from Hill's decision to give Usman Khawaja caught behind off Swann. This time Khawaja reviewed but for some reason, as yet unexplained, Kumar Dharmasena, the TV umpire, failed to see the fresh air between bat and ball or the fact that Hot Spot and the stump microphones had failed to spark. It was a bewildering decision which led James Sutherland, Cricket Australia's chief executive, to demand clarification from the International Cricket Council.

If Swann got lucky there, he deserved Rogers' wicket after slowing the left-hander's early charge to a crawl. With a cleverly set leg-side field, he pegged Rogers back until he played across a half-volley that turned enough to have him lbw from around the wicket.

With Clarke and Smith quick on their feet, Swann found it more difficult thereafter, unable to find a field setting to stem their combinations of shimmy and drive and the lay back and cut. He turned a few off the main part of the pitch but while that is normally a cause for joy for England, it will not be if Australia get past 450.

August 2 Michael Vaughan

The point of the Decision Review System is to save the game from the big mistakes made by umpires out in the middle. The problems in this series have been caused as much by human error as by the technology.

For the Usman Khawaja dismissal on Thursday everyone in the media centre and around the ground at Old Trafford could see he was not out but the third umpire did not overturn the decision.

Then later Australia's Steve Smith, I believe, was out caught behind off James Anderson. Hot Spot did not show up an edge but there was a noise. However, because the on-field umpire had given him not out, the third umpire did not have the evidence to overturn the decision.

Hot Spot did not pick up an edge but I do not trust it. Hot Spot is frustrating everyone at the moment. I am not sure how reliable it is. We all want to feel we are moving closer to getting more decisions right but this week the inventor of Hot Spot admitted it misses a few edges. That cannot be right. Perhaps we can use it in combination with the Snicko to make the system more accurate.

Overall I believe DRS is good for the game. It has moved cricket forward and we are getting more right decisions now. But we have to make sure the people who operate the system know the job. It sounds silly but we are in a situation where we need dedicated third umpires. It is a specialist job. At the moment one week an umpire is out in the middle, the next he is sat in a room surrounded by monitors.

It is a crucial role now. It is more frustrating when the third umpire makes a mistake. We understand human error out in the middle working in the heat of the moment, but find it hard to understand why a third umpire, with all the technology at his disposal, cannot come to the right decision every time.

A slight tweak to the system is required. I believe a team should have one review but not lose that review if they appeal an lbw and the verdict is umpire's call. A team is appealing because they believe the ball has pitched in line and is hitting the stumps. If a review shows it has pitched in line, and is clipping the stumps but remains umpire's call in the case of an original not out verdict, then I believe it is unfair for the bowling team to lose that review.

It is frustrating because later on a team may find it has no reviews left.

That happened to England here on the first day. The lbw

call on Smith from Graeme Swann was very tight. England lost a review and could not appeal an obvious mistake by Tony Hill later when he gave Smith not out to Stuart Broad, a ball which was hitting the middle of middle stump.

Hill should not have missed that. Likewise, Aleem Dar should not have missed the Broad edge at Trent Bridge.

This series has proved we need the best umpires standing in the big matches regardless of nationality. There are so many cameras at grounds it would be impossible for the umpires to get away with being biased, so have the best officials even if they are English or Australian.

August 2 Paul Hayward

Michael Clarke's rise to the captaincy earned him a label in his country's cricket literature as 'the second most powerful person in Australia'. After six Test defeats in a row, it looked less like a gift than a curse.

Impotence and isolation, not power, sprang to mind after the Lord's Test, where 'Pup' Clarke described Australia's batting as 'unacceptable' and seemed doomed to dash his own prodigious qualities on the rocks of this side's mediocrity. Providence seemed to steer him from working-class wonder boy to nation's leader, in the steps of Allan Border, Steve Waugh and Ricky Ponting, only to play a nasty trick on him, in the shape of Shane Watson, David Warner and assorted dilettantes or journeymen.

By the time Clarke took charge in 2011, the Baggy Greens had run out of talent, prompting Andrew Flintoff to tweet earlier in this series: 'Michael Clarke has been given the ulti-mate hospital pass captaining this team.' But then, on a hot Manchester day, the captain walked to the crease to capita-lise on the fine work of Chris Rogers, who scored 84, and unfurled his 24th Test century as Australia remembered how to bat with rigour.

Did the tourists end on 303 for three because the pres-sure was on or because it was taken off by the Trent Bridge and Lord's defeats? The conditions and this wicket begged to be exploited. No longer were their batsmen skittish, indisci-plined, over-eager. Rogers, 35, looked an opener of authority for the first time in this series.

Then Clarke emerged to serve up that classic spectacle – the captain's innings, which is often merely a high score that happens to have been posted by the leader.

Not this time. It was no good Clarke diagnosing weakness at the top of his order if he could not cure it himself. The title of Australia's 'only world-class player' is a nice ego-polisher, but it comes with obligations.

In England's opening two wins, attention fixed itself on Clarke messing up his umpire reviews, the wonder ball from James Anderson that took his wicket for a duck at Trent Bridge and the Lord's implosions. Until his triumphant unbeaten 125 here, though, Clarke had not passed 51 in four innings.

By the time he escaped London, the last of Australia's golden generation was disconsolate. 'Half of my problem I guess is that I walked into such a great Australian team that won as a habit and that was something I became accustomed to,' he said. 'I don't want that to change. At the moment we are not performing as well as I would like. We are letting everyone down at the moment with the way we are batting. Our bowlers are fighting hard, we are making them bowl every single day because we are not putting enough runs on the board.'

Manchester was a good place for a lad from Liverpool, in New South Wales, to turn this round, not through prima donna-ish sulks or tirades at less gifted colleagues, but with an innings of conviction and grace. The only active Australian Test batsman with an average higher than 50, Clarke is a delight when his feet are moving quickly, his shoulders are hunched over the shot and the ball is forced with smooth economy past diving fielders.

This was just such a day: a day of brightness and rebirth, on which the captain's pre-match bravado ('we can still win this series') seemed less hollow. One good day with the cudgel will not reverse England's superiority, but at least Australia's main problem has been cured for now. With 24 centuries in five-day cricket, he draws level with Greg Chappell in Australia's all-time list. Ponting, who handed over the crown of thorns, has 41. In the last two years alone, the anointed one has become the first Australian batsman to score four double centuries in a single calendar year and has also matched the Kim Hughes sequence of six consecutive Test losses.

Rogers called Clarke's innings 'massive', saying: 'I can't overstate it. He's such a key person. If he scores runs it makes it easier for those around him.'

The hard part is getting to the bottom of Clarke's status

as captain. The story about Simon Katich grabbing him by the throat during a row over the singing of Under the Southern Cross never quite goes away. Accounts of friction with Watson and other political rumbles suggest Clarke can never hope to secure the undivided adulation of this squad.

However painful it was for England's followers, ability on this scale should not be swallowed up by the ordinariness of others. An average team should not suck a star into its darkness. Rogers and Steve Smith both had their own stabs at redemption. They worked, as Australian batsmen should work, around the talismanic player. Clarke has a duty to his nation but also a right to fulfil his own talent.

August 2 Simon Hughes

They might call him Pup but Michael Clarke was a blood-hound on Thursday, sniffing out the opportunity of a hearty meal and never slackening his grip on the English bone.

With half his 24 Test hundreds scored abroad, he is also a dog who is happy to make a home in any conditions.

He took an important step before this third Ashes Test match by moving up to No 4 in the batting order. He averages only 20 in that position, with no major scores, compared to 65 at No 5 with 20 hundreds.

He was vacating his safe house for a more vulnerable place, but it was vital for the team that he took on the responsibility of shaping the innings, rather than – at No 5 – being shaped by it.

Coming in at 82 for two he looked overexposed at first,

and was uncertain before lunch, playing and missing, going hard at the ball and thick-edging runs on the leg side.

England still looked confident of hunting him down. He enjoyed some luck with an edge through the slips for four as he tried to leave a ball from James Anderson, and a faint edge on to his pad off Graeme Swann that just evaded leg slip.

The task of shoring up a shaky Australia batting order was weighing heavily on his aching back.

Normally a nimble batsman and a superb player of spin, he initially looked like a dancer wearing lead boots.

Slowly he remembered his steps: the stride back on to his stumps to play the turning delivery late, the shimmy up the pitch to caress, rather than crunch, the ball through extra cover against the spin.

As his muscle-memory rebooted, his footwork became silky and his timing sublime.

His range of movement – right back or two yards down the pitch – upset Swann's rhythm and forced him to try round the wicket.

Clarke bunted him back over his head, the field scattered and Swann went back over the wicket. Now Clarke had control and the runs began to flow.

He also remembered the leave – a crucial accessory on a flat pitch with trustworthy bounce because it obliges the pace men to try ploys other than merely bowling a channel outside off stump.

Clarke's influence was far reaching. Not only did it stabilise a listing vessel, it also set a course his young partner could follow.

Steve Smith, who appeared a walking wicket at first and had two lucky escapes, hung around and gradually found his rhythm, moving into better positions and playing the ball later.

He would not allow Matt Prior to goad him into risky adventure until it was safe to do so.

With his styled blond hair, his rock-star tattoo and his chirpy demeanour, Clarke is the antithesis of the archetypal Aussie captain, and his innings are decorated with sparkling shots and exquisite touches.

But the end product is all that really matters, and this was a performance to make all those old dogs of war – Chappell, Waugh, Border and Ponting – feel at least briefly proud to be Australian again.

Day Two
August 3 Derek Pringle

England (52-2) trail Australia (527-7d) by 475 runs

Alastair Cook moved into sixth place in England's pantheon of run-makers in Test cricket, but on a day when only one of five centurions was a batsman, his team will need him to leap another place if they are to avoid the follow-on target of 328.

Cook needs to add 87 to his overnight score of 36 to move ahead of Colin Cowdrey with 7,642 career runs, but he and his batsmen have made heavy work so far against Australia's bowlers, ending the second day on 52 for two after Peter Siddle struck twice in the final session of play.

It promises to be hard graft, but Cook and Jonathan Trott have never shirked from that, although Cook is suffering from a sore back that required him to take several pills during the final session.

The ball is spinning enough for Nathan Lyon, overlooked for the first two Tests in favour of Ashton Agar, to look as dangerous as Graeme Swann.

Cook almost fell in Lyon's first over, edging the ball into Brad Haddin's thigh. But whereas a similar rebound had gone to hand for England earlier in the day, this one fell short of Michael Clarke at slip.

Other than spin, the pitch holds few demons yet, as Clarke showed in scoring 187, his highest Test score against England.

His template of leaving the ball well outside off stump, picking off the bad deliveries and using the pace of the ball to score off the decent ones, is something Cook will have noted.

That and the fact that in the last Ashes Test here in 2005, which was drawn, both captains made hundreds.

So far, for England, only the bowlers have reached that milestone, with James Anderson, Stuart Broad, Tim Bresnan and Graeme Swann all conceding over a hundred runs apiece.

In fact, Anderson's nought for 116 were the worst figures of his Test career, a less than glorious homecoming for the leader of a pace attack rendered workmanlike by the largely intransigent surface.

At least Swann had the pleasure of a five-wicket haul, his 17th in Tests, while Broad reached his 200th Test wicket when he bowled Clarke off his mid-riff with one that bounced and cramped the batsman for room.

Broad spent 326 balls on 199 wickets but his elevation means England now have three members of the 200-club playing in a Test for the first time since February 1982, when Ian Botham, Bob Willis and Derek Underwood all played against Sri Lanka.

Siddle has 161 Test wickets, having added a curiously strokeless Joe Root and Bresnan, the nightwatchman.

After getting off the mark, Root was scoreless for 43 balls, pinned down by Shane Watson and Lyon.

When Clarke eventually turned to Siddle as his fifth choice Australia began to make progress as Root nicked one behind to Haddin.

Bresnan followed to the same combination, given out off the bottom edge after attempting a pull shot.

Unsure that the ball had made contact with his bat, he sought Cook's advice from the other end, only to find his captain unwilling to risk a review on a nightwatchman.

Bresnan looked unhappy, his grievance justified when TV replays showed daylight between bat and ball, not that such evidence guarantees a reprieve in the currently muddled world of the Decision Review System.

There was nothing muddled about Clarke's intentions when Australia resumed on 303 for three.

Since becoming captain, Clarke has gained an appetite for big hundreds.

Last year he made one triple century and two doubles, some going for any batsman, let alone one suffering from chronic back pain.

He did not reach those heights here but it was his highest score against England in his 23 Tests.

With Australia needing to win this match to keep the Ashes alive, he needed to score runs quickly but without resorting to great risk, a balance he and Steve Smith struck by targeting certain bowlers; Clarke picking on Bresnan, Smith on Swann, after they had seen off Anderson and Broad's opening salvo.

Bresnan came close to dismissing Clarke during one such burst.

Two flat-bat drives into an off-side field set for the shot saw the first drop just short of Kevin Pietersen at extra cover and the next parried by Swann, fielding closer on the same line.

Clarke then miscued a lofted drive just over Anderson's head at mid-off, before returning to the task of making England's bowlers suffer.

Smith's attempted assault on Swann proved far less successful, falling to the spinner's sixth ball of the day, trying to slog him to cow corner.

With just 11 runs needed for a first Test century it was an impetuous shot, though having enjoyed several lives on the opening day Smith probably felt fate was still on his side.

The wicket brought David Warner to the crease and the left-hander was greeted by a cacophony of boos.

It was a brutal introduction to Ashes cricket, but when you start punching opponents as angelic looking as Joe Root even Old Trafford's hardest turn into maternal protectors.

Sensing that the weight of public opinion was on his side,

Root seized the opportunity to join the chorus, firing off a few choice words at Warner before he had taken guard.

It was all a bit pantomime-predictable, though when Warner edged Swann to Jonathan Trott, via Matt Prior's knee, few expected him to consider a review, let alone persuade Clarke to let him waste one on an edge so obvious even Tony Hill had picked it up.

Clarke had no compunction in sending the deserving Chris Rogers packing the previous day, when he had sought his captain's opinion about the lbw Swann had won against him.

Conspiracy theories abound in cricket but it may not be too much of a coincidence that Warner has long been a staunch Clarke supporter in the dressing-room politics.

It remained out, as did Siddle's wild hack at Swann, which struck off stump.

At that point a quick wrap and England would have escaped bruised but not battered.

Unhappily for them, Haddin and Mitchell Starc added 97 in 117 balls, with Starc especially destructive.

August 3 Paul Hayward

To ascribe anti-hero urges to David Warner would be to overestimate his intellectual capacities. There is no evidence that Australia's most troublesome Test cricketer is playing the villain deliberately, so we are bound to see his career as one big diplomatic accident.

Some cartoon rogues go along with a panto script. Hate-figure status offers them something to kick against. Attention seekers are especially inclined to provoke the mob. Others just stumble into ridicule.

Warner, who threw away an Australian review despite clearly edging a Graeme Swann delivery to slip via wicket-keeper Matt Prior, is one of those who consider the sensible course of action for a moment or two and then do the opposite.

English cricket crowds have now set him up as a target for lampoonery.

They booed him to the crease and jeered him back to the pavilion on a day when Australia declared on 527 for seven. Taking their cue from the vast football ground just up the road they sang 'Who are you?' as he began his 16-minute stay at the crease and 'cheerio' as he plodded back after 10 balls.

The sensible course is not to abuse Australian journalists on Twitter. Warner goes the other way, earning himself a A$5,750 (£3,400) fine from Cricket Australia.

The sensible course is to observe Joe Root horsing around with a green and gold wig in a Birmingham bar and pass it off as youthful Pommie pluck. Warner goes the other way and throws a punch at the cocky Yorkshire cherub.

This 'despicable thing', to borrow the hyperbolic phrase used by James Sutherland, the Cricket Australia chief executive, brought Warner a suspension until the first Ashes Test at Trent Bridge, and thereby a doghouse spell with Australia A in southern Africa.

Under scrutiny, most exiled cricketers would probably cross the road to avoid any further bother while waiting for an Ashes recall. Warner goes the other way, and locks verbal horns with Thami Tsolekile, the South Africa A wicketkeeper:

news of which is bound to be blown up and held against him.

Then comes the big return. The big man is back in town for the Old Trafford Test, with Australia 2-0 down. Out goes Phil Hughes in favour of Root's assailant, who has the 'X-factor', according to Darren Lehmann, the Australia coach. But Lehmann reckoned without Warner's magnet-and-iron-filings relationship with trouble.

With Hughes sacrificed (and doubtless highly delighted by the bad boy's smooth return), Warner commits an act so devoid of reason that Ryan Campbell, the Adam Gilchrist understudy now coaching the Hong Kong national team, calls him a 'douche bag' in a tweet and adds: 'Sums u [sic] up I'm afraid.'

Warner was on five with Australia 365 for four when a Swann delivery clipped the thick edge of his bat, bounced off Prior's knee and nestled in Jonathan Trott's mitt at slip. There could be no doubt that he was out, except that Warner either convinced himself he had struck his pad with the bat or just decided to blow a raspberry at DRS by referring the dismissal for review.

Here Michael Clarke's role is interesting. Warner asked for his captain's opinion and was not discouraged from appealing, if the television pictures are any guide. Result: one of the most frivolous reviews in history ends with crushing confirmation of Swann's fourth wicket in the match. Australia, meanwhile, are all out of reviews.

Clarke has no reason to look out for Warner. The Walkabout punch in June is said to have dismayed Australia's captain. No leader of an embattled team is likely to trust a player who tries to banjo an opponent in a bar in the early hours of the morning.

Clarke could have overruled Warner's request for a review. Instead he watched him make a fool of himself. Not that any conscious disloyalty is implied.

To dwell on Warner's eccentricity on a day when Clarke reached 187, Steve Smith scored 89 and Brad Haddin and Mitchell Starc were unbeaten on 65 and 66 respectively might seem churlish. But there is no glossing over Root's sledging of his new sparring partner, which added further spice, or the stadium-wide hostility to Warner, who is now stuck with his villain tag.

Punching a Yorkshireman might not seem much of a crime at Lancashire's HQ, but the Old Trafford crowd, a boisterous lot, were standing right behind Root. Even old heads could not recall such a hostile reception for a cricketer.

Ricky Ponting was booed in this country, but with ironic undertones. Kevin Pietersen was hardly the darling of South African audiences on his return there with England. And Tony Greig took it in the neck here in 1977 for defecting to Kerry Packer.

Plainly Lehmann was deceived by Warner's 193 for Australia A in South Africa into thinking he would restore the runs to a fragile line-up.

Instead only Peter Siddle and Usman Khawaja scored fewer. The saviour role was performed by Rogers, Clarke and Smith before the tail wagged.

Lehmann's pragmatism in whistling Warner back to the starting side had no effect on the first two days of this match, except in providing the Old Trafford galleries with an appointed dunce to ridicule.

He will not shed the role easily. Only runs and application will allow this talented 26-year-old to raise the public's view of him. The trouble is: people who keep making bad calls seldom start making lots of good ones.

August 3 Simon Hughes

England have most bases covered in their support team, but perhaps what they could also do with is an ear specialist, so he could help all players detect whether the ball has flicked the bat or the pad.

I jest, but only partly. England's confusion over the night-watchman Tim Bresnan's attempted pull on Friday night cost them an important wicket. Luckily it did not cost them more. But the incident, and one involving David Warner earlier, emphasised the difficulty players (and umpires) have in deciphering whether a ball has been legitimately edged, and belies the notion that 'you always know when you have nicked it.'

Bresnan clearly had no idea, despite the fact that it looked from 70 yards away as if he had played over the top of the ball and replays proved it.

It had actually flicked the pocket of his trousers, four inches below the rather injudicious crooked swing of his bat. His partner, Alastair Cook, was apparently none the wiser, appearing to indicate that there was a noise but he could not be certain what it was. Some kind of special audio training is required for all concerned to train the ear to distinguish between a woody snick and a paddy flick.

The fact is batsmen do not always know if they have hit it, especially if the ball is whistling through at 85mph. You often cannot feel a thin edge on the blade, which leaves you relying on your eardrums. Then, depending on your attitude, the state of the match, and who is bowling, you can make a decision to look innocent or otherwise.

It happened to me in a one-day match at Lord's facing a fired-up Malcolm Marshall. We needed eight to win from 10 deliveries. I fenced at a fast ball outside off stump and missed it by a distance. There was a little click as it flew through head-high to the keeper, and the bowler and fielders all celebrated excitedly. But the umpire was unmoved and I was convinced I had not edged it. Eight to win off nine balls I said to myself. Then I thought, 'three of those balls are to be bowled by Malcolm Marshall'. And I walked off.

'Did you hit it?' my Middlesex colleagues asked me when I got to the dressing room. 'I don't know!' I said plaintively to howls of derision, and I still don't. Luckily we won the match.

Of course Stuart Broad knew he had edged the ball to slip via Brad Haddin's arm at Trent Bridge, it was a thick edge, but he is such a good actor he deserves an Equity card. The umpire did not pick it up though, nor did he detect what appeared to be a big edge from the bat of Steve Smith on Thursday afternoon. The problem is there are many noises when the batsman has a big drive at the ball: the batsman's spikes scraping on the ground, perhaps the brush of the bat against the pad on the way through, even the occasional flex of the bat springs themselves as the blade whooshes through the air.

I once dismissed Clive Rice caught behind after a loud click, which was later revealed on video to be the silver cross around his neck clanking against his visor as he swung the bat.

Warner's own impression of his fatal edge was understandably clouded by simultaneously hitting his pad with his bat, though it seemed almost incomprehensible that his partner, Michael Clarke, did not see the conspicuous evidence of ball ricocheting off bat and therefore tell him to go. What further complicates these incidents is the unpredictability of Hot Spot, which players are well aware does not always pick up thin snicks. Their default mode is to see what they can get away with.

However there have been so many errors in this series, and reviews wantonly wasted, that Bresnan took the noble option and sacrificed himself. Isn't that what nightwatchmen are meant to do?

August 3 Scyld Berry

England's supporters have to hope that Chris Tremlett running in to bowl on a practice pitch before the start of play at Old Trafford is a sight for sore eyes rather than a sight of sore thighs.

Going back to a pace bowler who turns 32 next month, who has not taken a Test wicket for two years and has suffered more than his share of injuries is – as England players now say with slightly nauseous regularity in press conferences – 'not ideal'. But someone has to beef up England's pace attack this winter, or even this summer.

There is something in this easy-paced pitch for the pace bowler who bends his back, as Peter Siddle proved when the shadows lengthened. But England's three seamers managed only two wickets on it for 338 runs.

Besides, not only were the figures of James Anderson, Stuart Broad and Tim Bresnan all too similar. So were their methods. This does not matter on English pitches that are offering lateral movement by one means or another, but three right-arm fast-medium bowlers on an Australian-style pitch – like this one – do not possess sufficient pace or variety between them. The combination, at least, is 'not ideal'.

And where is the growth potential? Superlative as James Anderson has become as a swing-and-seam expert, culminating in his 10-wicket masterclass against Australia at Trent Bridge, the graph of England's collective pace attack is going down, not up.

Since the start of last season, England's four main seamers – Anderson, Broad, Bresnan and Steven Finn – have taken 171 Test wickets at 33.6 runs each. Those are not great figures given that India has been the only venue hostile to pace bowling, and given Anderson's coming of age as a master craftsman.

Moreover, those figures include the two-Test series at home to New Zealand in May, when conditions offered lavish swing at Lord's and, to a lesser extent, Leeds and

England's opponents included such dogged but limited batsmen as Peter Fulton and Doug Brownlie. New Zealand compiled Bangladesh-like totals of 207, 68, 174 and 220.

Deduct that series at home to New Zealand and England's four main pace bowlers have been taking their wickets at 36 runs each since May 2012: that is in the home series against West Indies and South Africa, the away series in India and New Zealand, and this series against Australia to date.

On Friday Broad had his 200th wicket to celebrate when he aimed a short ball at exactly the right height for Michael Clarke: chest height. Broad tried to bring variety to the attack by resorting to the bouncer, though not to the cutters and slower balls which he has paraded as England's T20 captain.

Bresnan has been more accurate since returning this summer from his right elbow operation, and he was widely considered to have been the best of England's seamers on the first day. But when Clarke turned his attention to Bresnan and hammered three fours in a row – one a withering straight-drive – the bowler could not produce from his locker anything much more than steadiness.

England's original master plan for this summer had Finn tearing in on such easy-paced pitches, and knocking over Australian batsmen rather than bails at the non-striker's end. But Finn has not found the run-up that is right for him, or the style of bowling, perhaps because he has not found himself.

When he first appeared for England – and was just as good a bowler as he is now – Finn was his own man, quiet, fresh and keen off the field, suitably aggressive on it. The two personalities connected together in a coherent whole.

He knew what he wanted to do and, with polishing still to be done, did it.

Since then Finn seems to have gone corporate, the two personalities replaced by one that is personable but bland, on and off the field. He is bowling like a brand ambassador.

Hence England's need to revert to Tremlett – and maybe to fast-track Tymal Mills into this winter's touring party. Like Finn, Mills can exceed 90mph, but he is also left-handed and his bounce can be steep, as Graeme Swann's right forearm could testify after the England v Essex practice game.

The selection of Mills would be in the established tradition of England selecting a rookie quick bowler for Australia, such as Brian Statham, Alan Ward, Bob Willis, Graham Dilley, Norman Cowans – and Finn himself on Andrew Strauss's tour.

Not all were instant successes. But England's pace attack has to be beefed up this winter because here, as they say, it has been 'not ideal'.

Day Three

August 4 Scyld Berry

England (294-7) trail Australia (527-7) by 233 runs

England's batting has not gelled as a unit since 2011. On the few occasions they have made big totals, as in India, they have been the work of a couple of individuals.

As a result England are not immune from being defeated

over the last two days at Old Trafford and being pegged back to 2-1.

Michael Clarke, now the proud owner of an admirably disciplined attack, would prefer to give his bowlers a rest after England's first innings is terminated today because the fourth Test starts on Friday.

But the forecast of rain, and lack of time, may persuade him to enforce the follow-on in the hope that he can break the back of England's batting in their second innings before the backs of his pacemen.

Whether England fail to score 34 more runs and follow on, or if they have Monday to bat out, a less uneven distribution of labour than currently the norm would be welcome.

Kevin Pietersen scored his 23rd Test century, and he overtook Graham Gooch as the scorer of most runs for England in all formats, a wonderful achievement.

But the fact that he was out soon after reaching his hundred, and both Alastair Cook and Ian Bell were out soon after reaching their fifties, reflected the tenacity of Australia's bowling – and England's two-year failure to amass big totals.

The happiest part of England's day – in which they added 242 runs for the loss of five wickets – was the partnership between Pietersen and Bell. This was the sort of batting which would restore them to number one in the world Test rankings, if England's other batsmen can gel as well.

This partnership was not like the ones in the old days when Bell would cling to Pietersen's coat-tails. Pietersen was less forward than he used to be in his impulsive youth, and Bell much less backward.

This, for the first time, was a partnership between equals. Bell indeed outscored Pietersen by a small margin, 60 runs to his partner's 55. Pietersen drove two sixes off Lyon to Bell's one, but Bell played the shot of the partnership: a drive against Mitchell Starc that was nothing less than leathered through the covers.

For the last month Bell has been fulfilling the prophecy that he would become a great batsman. He has to keep going for the label to be attached permanently to his cricket bag but he seems to have found at last, aged 31, the missing ingredient. The perfectionist has shifted his focus to scoring runs, and technique is merely the means to that end.

With both batsmen exuding authority, England finally got out of second gear in the afternoon. Until Pietersen came in, their progress had been painfully laboured – 64 runs off 40 overs – and the Old Trafford crowd did not have the gall to sing 'If you are 2-0 up, stand up!' as they did when Pietersen and Bell were matching each other stroke for imperious stroke.

The ploy of sending in Tim Bresnan as nightwatchman on Friday evening had contributed to England's innings congealing and added to the weight on Cook's sore back. Sending in a neo-allrounder like Bresnan with half-an-hour to go was not a bad move, but sending in someone who had just bowled 33 overs in hot weather was, for his shot-selection was bound to be loose.

For the second Test running Jonathan Trott was out when caught in two minds: to play or not to play. Trott does not do tentative, normally, but the big score has refused to come

– and in the last two years his Test batting average has been no more than 37.

Perhaps Trott was also affected more than anybody else in the England side by the implosion in the Champions Trophy final, for his last chance of a global trophy has probably gone.

Thus the stage on which Pietersen made his entrance was rickety. He had to supply the impetus himself, as Cook was hanging on much like Chris Tavare had done on the Saturday of the Old Trafford Test in 1981, when Ian Botham had walked out to score 118 in his finest feat of batting – his 149 in the Headingley Test having been hitting.

And just as Botham had been quiet at first, the Australians' decision to resort to the short ball brought Pietersen to life. It was not quite so spectacular as Dennis Lillee bouncing Botham downwind and getting hooked into Warwick Road station, but Pietersen still put away two consecutive short balls from Starc: one a front-foot hook, the second inimitable Pietersen.

The parallels between Pietersen and Botham did not extend much further, partly because they could not. The new Old Trafford, with its reoriented square, has too long a boundary for anyone to attempt a hook for six when the bowling is from the new pavilion end.

Once Cook had been caught glancing down the legside after four hours of hard labour, Pietersen had Bell for lively company.

Together they hit Nathan Lyon out of the attack, taxing his four overs after lunch for 29 runs – after the whole morning had yielded only 67. The chant about 2-0 up rang out with conviction, and upon the waves of patriotic fervour Pietersen reached the harbour of his first Test century at Old Trafford.

But the Australian bowling was simply too sturdy and determined to deteriorate under assault. Bell was undone by the tourists' attack-leader, Ryan Harris, who seamed the ball back through Bell's backward defensive – forward would have been more appropriate – to hit the top of offstump.

Jonny Bairstow never got in before he got out, edging Starc. Pietersen dried up, playing and missing against Shane Watson in particular, and the longer his innings went on after reaching three figures the scratchier it became.

Partly through being fuller of collective length, the Australian pace bowlers have found more lateral movement, especially with the new balls. It is just as well for England they have a two-game cushion. As for the return series this winter, they now know it will be a different kettle.

August 4 Steve James

It was a defining day for England. That might seem rather strange to be offering that observation about a side 2-0 up in the series, but it was the day on which their big guns simply had to fire for the first time in this series in order to rebuff the brave Australian fightback.

Captain Alastair Cook did moderately well in that regard. But Jonathan Trott did nothing of the sort, uncertain whether to play or not, and poor Jonny Bairstow is no gun at this level yet.

The scene was set for big Kev, the biggest of the guns. And, despite a start to his innings that was scarcely fathomable in its nervousness, he fired all right, making a century and easily grabbing the headlines.

England needed that, but the truth is that at no stage did he bat better than Ian Bell, who has been firing all series.

Bell did not make a century but he made 60 runs of such elegance that we could have been watching David Gower batting in a mirror.

If he were a player of more extroversion, they might already be preparing a DVD entitled 'Belly's Ashes'. But they will not.

Doubtless, there will still be some who doubt Bell's credentials as a top-ranker in the batting pantheon, even though he has already made two centuries in this series, and three in consecutive Ashes Tests before this.

For he is a player who attracts strong judgments. He once had a reputation for being mentally soft, for piggybacking colleagues' hundreds earlier in an innings. And he has struggled to shed such perceptions.

No matter that he has played some truly gutsy innings to go with the aestheticism, not least in saving the Cape Town Test on the 2009-10 tour to South Africa. His rearguard action in Auckland this winter was not too shabby, either.

Yes, many of his runs have come in the calmer waters at No 5 and No 6 in the order, but Steve Waugh hardly used to rush to the front of the batting queue and no one called him soft.

And Bell can push up, as he showed so brilliantly when

making 159 at No 3 after an injury to Trott against India at Trent Bridge in 2011.

Ashes series tend to define the cricketers on both sides, and they are remembered accordingly – goodness, Mike Gatting only won two Tests as England captain and they just happened to be against Australia in 1986-87.

So even if there is to be no DVD, surely Bell has now done more than enough in Ashes cricket to be recalled with the very best.

He has travelled far since a chastening Ashes debut eight years ago, when his finest match was actually here where he made 59 and 65.

Otherwise he made scores of 6, 8, 6, 21, 3, 3 0 and 0 in that series. But that was a great Australian side. Since then Bell has been making his own rocky journey towards greatness.

He could easily have been out for nought, though. Interestingly Mitchell Starc, the tall left-armer, immediately went around the wicket to him.

Most right-handed batsmen would dread a left-arm seamer attacking them from over the wicket early on. But that is only when the ball is swinging, and the possibility of an lbw verdict has the umpire's index finger twitching.

But the ball was not swinging and so Starc altered his line of attack. And he should have found reward. He beat Bell and the ball went through to wicketkeeper Brad Haddin, who appealed plaintively.

Meanwhile, around Haddin nobody moved and nobody appealed. Haddin was alone in the audience laughing at a stand-up comedian.

Now everyone was laughing at him, including skipper Michael Clarke at slip. Except they should not have been. Haddin was right. His instinct had been sound.

He thought Bell had edged the ball. And he had. Technology proved as much later on.

Observers and commentators often talk about batsmen being in form. I do not believe in that. Yes, there may be periods when one's technical competence dips below that required to score runs consistently, but that is different.

And it does not happen half as often as is thought by some batsmen – especially the modern player who rushes to watch a video replay the moment he is dismissed.

More usually batsmen are in luck. They go through periods where fortune is their faithful friend, and so they form a beautiful relationship called confidence. Remember that Bell was probably caught at Lord's in the last Test, but was reprieved by technology's limitations in that respect. Here he got lucky, and duly hit the next ball to the cover boundary for four. He was away.

And how. His driving to that cover boundary off both front and back feet was exquisite, and he lofted Nathan Lyon over mid-off for a six that screamed ease.

But he was eventually defeated by a beauty of a break-backer from Ryan Harris. With that Australia had hope, raised further by Pietersen's later departure.

Nothing definitive yet then. The battle rages, except about Bell and Pietersen's status amongst the very best.

August 4 Paul Hayward

Two classic English team men dropped a notch here on Survival Saturday.

Graham Gooch and Alec Stewart, No1 and No2 in the all-forms runs list, fell to second and third in the rankings as Kevin Pietersen became the most prolific English batsman in all types of the game, passing Gooch's 13,190 on a day perfectly set up for a limelight-seeking batsman to present himself as the saviour.

Gooch and Stewart were band-of-brothers types. National unity was their starting point.

Pietersen – L'Etranger – is the archetypal individual stranded in a collective.

But that works well enough for England when the chance arises for their gifted No4 to answer the call of destiny: or at, least, the call that originates in his own head.

Few cricketers have ever set out for work with such a conscious desire to attain greatness.

When it goes wrong, Pietersen can appear about as integrated in society as Holden Caulfield in *The Catcher In The Rye*.

When it works, he writes the day's lead story with his skill, physical authority and sense of occasion.

With England imperilled in this third Ashes Test, Pietersen raised his bat to the Manchester crowd to mark his 23rd Test century – his fourth against Australia – after lifting an uppercut to third man to reach three figures off 165 balls.

There are people in this England set-up who would not care if they never had to talk about Kevin again. Few, though, would choose to go into an Ashes series without the England batsman most capable of turning a game on its head through sheer bravura. Never mind that Pietersen's talent walks the line between extravagance and self-indulgence.

The figures say he will win you a Test often enough to compensate for the political distractions. Or save one for you, if the act of rescuing it offers him a chance to feel really good about himself.

However much he brands himself, or is drawn to celebrity's flame, his true milieu is the one that made him: Test cricket, where he has time to stretch his majesty across a genuinely national event.

His five-day debut, after all, was the Lord's Test of 2005, for which he was picked ahead of Graham Thorpe.

His 158 in the concluding Oval Test that year was a statement by which he would always be measured. Brilliant, bold and bullying, that innings gave rise to an expectation that followed him all the way to Old Trafford eight years on.

A lot happened in between. The texting scandal, the loss of the England captaincy and a tug of war over his limited-overs career have cast many shadows over his batting, not to mention assorted injury problems, the latest of which (a sore calf) was only narrowly overcome in time for this match.

There has never been an athlete in any sport – however great – who has remained immune from doubt after periods of poor form or inactivity. In Pietersen's early demeanour at the crease you can see not only a strange habit of flicking the bat around outside off stump but also a fear of what life will be like when cricket no longer provides an opportunity for him to post his name in lights.

For several years now he seems to have been driven back to England colours by a terror of losing his big stage in life.

And again he began an innings skittishly, as if unsure of his ability to assert his talents.

England's best batsman in this Test has thrown his wicket away plenty of times without seeming to hate himself for it.

Equally he starts out like a man petrified by the thought of failure.

When he settles, the bat straightens, his shoulders lift and he grows in size and stature. He becomes a physical threat to bowlers. A bludgeoning quality enters his shot making.

Across England, people rush in from gardens to see him pirouetting at the crease.

The prospect of a big Pietersen innings remains thrilling, even if there is the sense that it could end any time, through slackness or over-ambition.

Aggression reached its peak for him in the 63rd over when he hammered consecutive sixes off Nathan Lyon to bring up his 50. The first soared over long-on. The second sailed over long-off. With this flurry he passed Colin Cowdrey's aggregate of 7,624 to go seventh on the England list of Test run scorers.

There was an escape, too. There always is. Australia declined to review a Shane Watson delivery that struck Pietersen on the pads and would have hit the stumps. He had scored 62.

A 115-run partnership off 218 balls with Ian Bell was attractive for its contrasts: Bell, the confident, artistic ball-steerer, Pietersen, the big hitter, always searching for the right blend of power and precision.

But when Pietersen fell lbw to Mitchell Starc on 113 England still needed 48 to avoid the follow on. So a fine innings fell just short of epic status. It did, though, confirm Pietersen as a major player in this series, after his tasty 64 at Trent Bridge.

As noticeable as the blows themselves was the warmth of the send-off by this Old Trafford crowd as he left the field in the early evening light. Cricket loves a colossus – an aggressor – and on that front Pietersen can still deliver.

August 4 Michael Vaughan

Alastair Cook and Michael Clarke have one thing in common. They are extremely good batsmen who know how to bat with the pressure of captaincy – calming the dressing room by the way they play.

Cook is more of a grinder who likes to wear the opposition down, whereas Clarke has the ability to take on spinners by manoeuvring his feet into position, but they have both worked out their methods of scoring runs while carrying the burden of captaincy.

Where they differ is in their tactics out in the middle, Cook generally likes to allow his bowlers to set their own fields.

He stands at first slip and allows James Anderson, Stuart Broad, Tim Bresnan and Graeme Swann to control the fielders.

Bowlers like to shore up an end when they set fields. The England team analyst will be telling them that the more maidens and dots they bowl, the more opportunities will come your way.

I would say that for England to move up to the next level they have to read pitch conditions better and adapt, particularly when it is flat and the ball is not swinging.

On days one and two at Old Trafford there was an argument to say that they could have been more creative and inventive. They bowled conventional, top of off stump, to orthodox fields.

It was crying out for an unorthodox approach. Go short as you would in the subcontinent. Be aggressive with a third man and a man on the hook to someone like Clarke, who has been out to the short ball in the past.

Alternatively bowl full and straight. Bowl yorkers for three overs, or you could go wide of off stump and get Clarke to chase one with seven-two off-side field. You need four or five plans when the opposition bat well on a flat pitch. England did not do enough to create a different environment for Australia.

Clarke is a mover and shaker. He is what I call a funky captain. He likes to be proactive. He uses frequent bowling changes to create new angles, never letting the batsman settle.

He creates new field settings and invents catching positions that might force an error in a shot or create an opportunity for a wicket. Sometimes he can be too funky. Sometimes the situation demands orthodox play. If you had a captaincy gauge I would say Clarke swings to being too unorthodox, Cook the opposite.

If I was being critical of my own captaincy then I would

say I was like Clarke and too unorthodox at times. To be the best captain in the world you have to have the right balance. Realise when to think differently and when to allow the pitch to do the talking. That is the skill as a captain.

The best captain I ever saw as a player was Stephen Fleming. He always asked questions. First and foremost his idea was to have six or seven fielders in positions where he thought the ball would go and he could take a wicket. The rest would be there to block out runs. You need two sets of fielding units when being aggressive. On a flat wicket you need catchers in place to get wickets but fielders in place to stop runs. A theory I used on good pitches was not to allow the batsmen easy boundaries.

I would regularly put the cover point on the boundary, which would then free up the man at extra cover, who could be in tighter to take a catch if there was a mistimed drive. Boundary riders allow you to have more catching positions. Ultimately this has been a fascinating Test match played on a true wicket.

It has something for everyone. Seamers who bowl with pace and consistency have done well but you have been found out if you do not bowl at 85mph or if as a spinner you fail to put enough revolutions on the ball.

Ultimately this series could be decided by Swann being the stand-out spinner. He has 18 wickets, while Australia's three spinners between them have taken six in three Tests played on dry, dusty wickets. I bet Clarke goes to bed at night wishing he had a certain Shane Warne in his ranks. Then again we would all have liked that to be the case.

Day Four

August 5 Derek Pringle

Australia (527-7d & 172-7) lead England (368) by 331 runs

A draw will be enough for England to retain the Ashes on Monday and history suggests that they are at the right venue to achieve it.

Old Trafford has hosted 29 Ashes Tests prior to this one and 14, almost 50 per cent, have ended in deadlock, the highest percentage of all the main Test grounds at home.

Add to that today's forbidding forecast, which is predicting solid rain until lunchtime and then showers in the afternoon, and Michael Clarke and his bowlers could have under two sessions to take the 10 wickets they need to keep the Ashes alive.

On a pitch that has misbehaved about as much as the scholars at Manchester Grammar school, an urn-retaining draw is looking the likely outcome for Alastair Cook's team. Cook and his team could surprise us by going for the runs, but they do not need to.

England once made 315 in the fourth innings to beat Australia at Headingley in 2001, but the series had already been lost and a cavalier attempt, led by Mark Butcher's fine hundred, was the noble option once Adam Gilchrist had declared.

If an England win is unlikely, they will also be keen to avoid the fate of their predecessors here earlier that summer when Pakistan took their last 10 wickets for 176 on the final day.

Such collapses usually happen only if the ball is swinging or spinning lavishly, which it has yet to do in this match, even if Australia have the bowlers, Mitchell Starc and Nathan Lyon, with the requisite skills. Clarke would have hoped to have utilised them and his other bowlers at England in their second innings already, but bad light and then rain brought a premature close to play on Sunday after the match had been delicately poised at tea.

At that stage all three results remained a possibility, but when the umpires took the players off at 4.25pm, after light levels had fallen despite the floodlights, it elevated the likelihood of the draw above the other two results.

The period of bad light lasted only 30 minutes before rain arrived to provide a more conclusive reason for play to be suspended, but it was long enough for Clarke to show his frustration. The light and conditions became the sole remit of the umpires three years ago.

Before that, they would judge it, then offer it to the batsmen.

At that point they would take a reading, which would dictate when they returned or, should the batsmen have stayed on, made a subsequent offer to them.

Clarke obviously wanted to play on and increase Australia's lead to around 350, which would enable him to keep men around the bat for his spinners.

He could have done so, had Cook been prepared to bowl spin at each end, but when Marais Erasmus asked the

England captain if he would consider the option he declined, as you might expect with the Ashes at stake, and play was suspended.

In explanation to Sky Sports, Tony Hill, Erasmus's on-field colleague, said he had been struggling to track the ball when standing at square leg. That is difficult to do with fast bowlers in good light, especially for a 62-year-old whose eyesight is not going to be as sharp as that of the batsmen.

Hill also said that play could have continued if England had been prepared to bowl spin, though his logic appeared flawed when he said that they had gone off because of the safety of all parties, including the fielders and umpires.

If you can understand why the batsmen, who were willing to waive their rights to being protected anyway, would be more imperilled by fast bowling, it should not have made any difference to the others. The crowd, sensing a dramatic final session, booed the officials. The use of floodlights, which has kept play going longer than in the past, has also created confusion.

It used to be that play ceased once the artificial light, which does not much enhance the sighting of a red ball out of a white sight screen, took over from the natural, a moment judged once the players cast multiple shadows on the ground. But that protocol has gone and it is now left to the umpires' discretion when to halt play.

If Clarke's anger was understandable, and not just because the break delayed his declaration, the light would have needed to improve a great deal for England to have batted against the new ball.

Instead, that opening salvo is likely to provide the big moment on Monday, should play get under way, as the older ball has demanded nothing but hard graft. England's deliberate dallying, which slowed their over rate to 12.2 an hour, would not have pleased Clarke either, but every team would have done the same once they had avoided the follow-on.

Not that Clarke was likely to have enforced it anyway, preferring to rest his bowlers and allow the pitch to wear some more before trying to bowl England out for a second time.

Having begun the day 34 runs short of the 328 required to make Australia bat again, England needed some application from Matt Prior and Stuart Broad, the two batsmen taking up cudgels. They did not disappoint, seeing their team past the follow-on target before Broad became Lyon's first victim of the match.

Prior then farmed the strike, reducing Australia's lead to 159, until he was last man out. Then, after Australia negotiated the new ball to minimal alarm through David Warner and Chris Rogers, it was a case of slowing their opponents' advance.

Taking regular wickets helped them keep the charge to below five runs an over, the most symbolic dismissal being Joe Root's running catch at deep square leg to get rid of David Warner off Tim Bresnan's bouncer. Warner will be ecstatic if he can turn the tables on Root on Monday, but there will have to be some play first and Manchester's weather is famous for thwarting that.

August 5 Paul Hayward

Manchester: so much to answer for. If the Met Office forecast is correct this Old Trafford Test is dead and the Ashes are retained.

This being England, the two sides could yet wake to stone-splitting sun, and Australia could still motor to Durham 2-1 down, but the chances are that this odd series ended with a stoppage for bad light while floodlights blazed across the pitch.

For a series bedevilled by doubt about the decision review system – and the humans running it – a bizarre dispute over light was an apt way to bring the weekend to a close. In truth it was immaterial. While Australia's batsmen still fumed about the umpires' decision to force them off (Michael Clarke, the captain, was understandably desperate to continue), English drizzle scattered the 26,000 crowd and raised the grim probability that this series will be settled by a draw, after just 14 days.

If so, we must prepare our goodbyes: to the contest, but not the cricket, which heads off to the 'desolate' North East before concluding at the Oval, scene of the great showdowns of 2005 and 2009, when both sides were superior to the ones we have seen trade blows at Trent Bridge and Lord's.

Eight years ago, England hurled a fearsome four-man attack at Ricky Ponting's Australia. Distance lends even more enchantment to the bowling of Andrew Flintoff, Simon Jones, Steve Harmison and Matthew Hoggard, and to the emergence of Kevin Pietersen, author of that wonderful innings of 158 in south London.

The core of that winning side was still intact in 2009, despite an intervening whitewash in Australia, as Andrew Strauss headed the scoring charts with 474, Stuart Broad took 18 wickets and Graeme Swann established himself as England's senior spinner.

This time, an England of multiple personalities (imperious one week, fragile the next) are within sight of dispatching an Australia team derided as one of the worst to leave those southern shores. Here at Old Trafford the rolling obituary for the Baggy Greens was halted first by a journeyman, Chris Rogers, seizing his last chance with a defiant knock of 84, and then by Michael Clarke's 187 in an Australian total of 527 for seven declared: their first of real authority in this series.

Too late, probably. The Lord's collapse (128 and 235) was prefigured by Australia stumbling to 117 for nine in their first innings at Trent Bridge before a miraculous 98 by 19-year-old Ashton Agar applied a romantic sheen to their underwhelming efforts. At Lord's they were crushed by 347 runs. No Australian batsman made it beyond 54. Agar went for 142 without taking a wicket, which cost him his place here in Manchester, where Rogers talked well about how it felt it to be a laughing stock.

If Australia roused themselves in this third Test it was because winning the toss gave them the whiff of runs on a benign pitch. With Rogers to the fore, they batted with discipline and rigour. 'The pressure was off a bit and we felt a bit more free to play our shots,' said Rogers, giving the game away. With the series virtually lost, Australia were already in rebirth mode. They could take heart from the depth of their batting and the bowling of Mitchell Starc, though quite why Clarke displays so little faith in Peter Siddle as a game-changing wicket-taker is beyond explanation.

Some have found the drawn-out phases of this Test a bit of a turn-off. When we look back, however, there will be plenty to commend it. First, Warner's emergence as Ashes cartoon villain was a throwback to the Seventies. In his faintly hapless way, he seemed to enjoy it as much as the crowd.

England used Warner as a dartboard as he swung and swiped his way to a useful score that helped Australia run up a lead of 331. There have been other pleasures in this Test. Ian Bell's 60 featured some sublime strokes, all wrist and balance and precision. Kevin Pietersen's 113 restored the link to 2005 and re-affirmed his big-game qualities. Purists might prefer Bell's artistry. But English cricket still has no greater selling point than Pietersen's athletic belligerence. The crowds in Durham and at the Oval will hope to see plenty more.

Alastair Cook, Jonathan Trott, Jonny Bairstow and Matt Prior still chase a big Ashes score, though Cook's 62 here was a move in the right direction.

Bairstow is batting without conviction. This series has lurched about a bit, with only the tense finish at Trent Bridge entering the book of classic Ashes melodramas. It will disappoint, too, if the battle for the urn itself (the raison d'etre, after all), ends in the rain, with two Tests left. So the neutral hopes for a fifth-day reprieve: a Monday of demonic Australian bowling and English stoicism.

The real contest may come in the return series, in Australia this winter, when Clarke's team will have addressed their deepest flaws. If DRS can be properly managed, there is no chance of an Ashes series ever dropping below the level of compelling. The proof is that you hate the thought of it ending.

August 5 Simon Hughes

Michael Clarke is one of the more enterprising captains, but he made a crucial mistake at the start of play on Sunday that probably cost his team their last chance of winning back the Ashes.

With England still needing 34 runs to save the follow-on, and only three wickets left, he opened the bowling with Nathan Lyon from one end, and Ryan Harris – rather than Peter Siddle – from the other.

Half an hour later Matt Prior and Stuart Broad were still together and had given England a 10-run lead. With rain forecast for later in the match, which duly arrived at 5pm, Australia's best and probably final hope of victory and keeping the series alive had gone.

Such situations used to be so straightforward for Australian captains. On a wearing fourth-day pitch they could throw the ball to Glenn McGrath and Shane Warne. Few runs would be yielded, there would be wicket-taking deliveries aplenty and a generally frosty atmosphere round the bat to make the batsman's life as uncomfortable as possible.

Success was pretty much guaranteed. In the decade and

a half that pair played together they enforced the follow-on 13 times.

Clarke has no such luxury. Few captains do. But he seems to harbour a strange reluctance to use Siddle, the best bowler in this Australian team, as his enforcer. Instead he is generally put on as an afterthought, once the others have had a go.

Perhaps he is just one of those bowlers who does an honest job and does not draw attention to himself. He is not excessively tall or excessively strong or excessively quick. He does not make the ball move dramatically or possess a wicked slower ball or bowl searing bouncers. He does not have tattoos of his children's names visible all over his body.

He is more sidle than Siddle, his presence almost unnoticed by the captain, by the spectators, and by the opposition. And yet he has 165 Test wickets at an average of a little more than 28, and is the fifth-best Test bowler in the world according to the rankings – higher than James Anderson or Graeme Swann.

Siddle is essentially a no-frills, old-fashioned, line-and-length merchant. A willing workhorse, to use a horrible, undervaluing phrase. He perennially bustles in to bowl, jumps into a solid, unspectacular delivery stride and sends the ball zipping down the other end at a decent, though not devastating, lick. A vegan, he is not sustained by that traditional fast bowlers' staple of raw steak, but instead gets through the day eating a dozen bananas.

But his stamina is excellent and his deliveries are invariably in the interrogation area, asking awkward questions.

'Should I play or should I leave?' 'Forward or back?' 'Is it a leg-cutter or a nip-backer?'

In fact, he has only one basic delivery. Brisk, seam up, released from close to the stumps. Occasionally he steps out a touch wider and brings the same ball down from a slightly different angle. And that is essentially it. The only sign of individuality is the baring of his teeth, with just a hint of wild dog about the jaw line, after a near miss.

This combination has been good enough to dismiss many of the premier willow-wielders in the game: Kevin Pietersen and AB de Villiers (six times each), Alastair Cook (five times), Hashim Amla and Sachin Tendulkar (four times each).

In this Investec Ashes series Siddle has already seen off 15 England batsmen at a cost of only 22 runs apiece. He is like one of those 'invisible' drones sneaking under the radar. Why Clarke did not begin with him on Sunday only he knows.

Harris, who seems to start a series well and then go down-hill, was preferred and offered up a pleasant half-volley to Prior second ball which he eagerly drilled for four. A short delivery lacking genuine venom was dispatched in his next over.

Lyon beat Broad's bat occasionally with his off-breaks but lacked consistency and 25 runs had been gleaned from five overs. Broad was now down Harris's end. Shaky against the short ball, he required roughing up. But after one solitary bouncer that struck Broad's shoulder, Harris fed his strength outside off stump and was walloped for three boundaries.

Are quick bowlers so conditioned to their 'fifth-stump'

approach that they cannot bowl a decent bumper any more? Clarke decided to withdraw Harris after four overs that had cost 27 runs.

Once Broad had walked – shock horror – to a thin edge off Lyon, it took the newly introduced Siddle only three deliveries to find a chink in Graeme Swann's defence, and, not long afterwards, he winkled out Prior to finish the innings. But by then it was probably too late for Australia. It is probably too late for Siddle as well. Good bowlers in bad teams are rarely celebrated.

Day Five

August 6 Derek Pringle

England (368 & 37-3) draw with Australia (527-7 & 172-7)

A Test drawn because of rain is a drab way for England to retain the Ashes in record time, but Alastair Cook and his team will take them while the going is good after Australia at last found enough bite to draw English blood.

A wet Monday in Manchester is nobody's ideal backdrop for cricketing glory and only a smattering of bedraggled fans hung on to glimpse Cook spraying the champagne.

Compared to the singing and cheering hordes in Melbourne 2½ years ago and the Oval in 2009, it was as if he had won best cake at the village fete.

This was the third successive series that England have held the Ashes, a feat last accomplished from 1953-56, when

Peter May's team also retained the urn at Old Trafford, albeit on the back of Jim Laker's 19 wickets.

That team also won the series, a result that Cook's side, 2-0 up with two to play, will want to seal in the next Investec Test which begins in Chester-le-Street on Friday.

To that end, and possibly to rotate one or two of the pace bowlers, Chris Tremlett and the in-form Graham Onions have been added to the squad.

It took England 14 days to retain the Ashes, the fewest needed at home in the era of five-day Tests.

When timeless Tests were the vogue, a fortnight was scarcely enough time to muster two results but in 2013 it has proved ample for an efficient, rather than brilliant, England against an underpowered Australia.

Australia's batting infirmity in the first two Tests was the main reason for the swift settlement, though they rallied well enough here to suggest that the remaining Tests in this rubber, and the return series this winter, should be a tougher proposition, especially if their main pace bowlers manage to stay fit.

After a largely dry morning in which England were made to look distinctly vulnerable, rain returned three balls after lunch to have the final word.

When play did begin on the final day, after a wet night and morning, it looked as if England had been caught on the hop, with many of the team arriving just 45 minutes before the rescheduled start at 11.30am.

For this most professional of England teams a warm-up and practice session of at least an hour would be mandatory, especially on a day when Australia would be throwing every-thing at them.

Yet team director Andy Flower denied they had been caught napping.

'We never pay that much attention to forecasts,' he said. 'There was only ever going to be indoor facilities available for warm-up, so we just had a quiet one and the batsmen had a hit.

'Then we had to go out and fight on a pitch that had worn significantly, which was never going to be easy.'

Not for the first time this summer, England's top order looked shaky, as Ryan Harris and Peter Siddle added frenetic purpose to their propulsions.

Swinging the ball, Harris had Cook lbw to one that shaped in.

For some reason Cook, after a consultation with Joe Root in which the truth would have tested any young man's loy-alty, reviewed the decision.

One suggestion was that he did it to waste time, but if he felt the ball was askew his radar was clearly not working, which might at least explain his poor showing this series.

Jonathan Trott has also struggled, meaning England's rapid retention of the urn has been achieved without much from the two main run-scorers of the last campaign.

Trott was almost lbw to Harris when on nine, but the umpire's call on the Decision Review System saved him. Hawk-Eye showed the ball striking the outside half of leg stump.

His head is toppling over too far to the off side, which

unbalances him and changes the geometry of bat and body working together.

It almost led to his downfall to Harris and was definitely at fault when he tickled Siddle down the leg side and was caught by Brad Haddin.

Afterwards, Flower predicted that Trott's experience would see him through the remainder of the series.

'Trott has not made heavy runs yet, but he has made an impact on our good position in the series,' he said.

'A guy with his record and his experience, we'd expect to make big contributions in the last two Tests.'

Kevin Pietersen's return to form in the first innings would have been a welcome sight but his record in second innings for England is patchy – his 68 in the first Test at Trent Bridge is his sole second-innings half-century in two years.

His dismissal, caught behind groping at one off Siddle, prompted first a review, after Tony Hill had given him out, and then ire, after the television umpire upheld the decision on minimal evidence.

It might have been a pivotal moment had Root also been held by Michael Clarke off Siddle and the weather stayed dry, but its poignancy will be limited to just another misgiving over Hot Spot, which has been discredited in this match.

Root was let off at Lord's, too, when Clarke and Haddin watched an edge off Shane Watson pass between them.

England have been 30 for three or worse in three of their past four innings, poor starts that would have been made even worse had Root been caught.

He and Bell held fast long for enough to see England past

lunch, when the conclusive rain arrived to seal Australia's fate.

Two Australian teams of recent vintage managed to retain the Ashes in 11 and 13 days, in 2001 and 2002-3, but those contained several all-time greats.

This one is more modest but their ability to come back from their abject showing at Lord's should not be under-estimated and might yet have a bearing on the rest of the series.

August 6 Paul Hayward

Captain Cook has made a big discovery with his conquest of Australia. Leading your country in an Ashes series is every bit as stressful as the pantheon of former England captains in the media could have told him.

But so blessed is Alastair that he retained the urn without shining as a batsman or strategist.

England cricket captains are a special bunch. On any given day in the press box you might run into six or eight. All were fine players elevated to perhaps the most onerous leadership job in sport. Running your own life in an Ashes series looks hard enough. But you are required as well to run everybody else's.

In the simplest sense Cook struck the captaincy jackpot on a soggy day in the North West. He retained the Ashes in 14 days. With a little help from Manchester's climatic incontinence, he survived Australia's huge first-innings total of 527 for seven declared to escape with a draw that adds a grand Ashes achievement to his winning start as captain against India.

Who could find fault with that? No one, but there is a case for thinking his own game is suffering in line with a tradition of England captains finding the job exhilarating at first and then an intellectual and emotional burden.

Australia are improving. England are not. The circus swings east to Durham with a question unresolved. Can Cook return to being the talisman of this side while helping those around him to the two further wins that would strangle the Australian rebirth? Clear thinking, and its opposite, is sharply visible in these contests.

For all his admirable qualities, Cook has yet to nail the captain's role against Australia, when the need to win is so pronounced – and the opposition so hostile – that the brain is bound to freeze at first.

The captain's frivolous review of a clear lbw off Ryan Harris when he was still on nought in England's rocky second innings was the clearest sign yet that responsibility is weighing on him heavily.

Cook must have known he was out. So must Joe Root at the non-striker's end. But the leader still subjected himself to the ignominy of throwing away a review for purposes unknown. Vanity? He is not that type. To waste time? Surely England were not so desperate that they needed to burn five minutes? The simplest explanation is that Cook was in the mental vortex known to everyone who has worn the general's tunic in Ashes cricket.

The message it sent to the England dressing room was

that Australia had broken through Cook's psychological defences. What followed raised doubts about England's preparations for this final day.

Anticipating an easy vigil in the rain, they arrived in a Durham state of mind. Jonathan Trott, whose form has deserted him, was out chasing a Harris delivery down leg side and then Kevin Pietersen grumbled his way back to the pavilion after also being caught behind. England were now 27 for three and suddenly desperate for rain.

Cook is such an exalted player with the bat that he was naturally expected to transfer that sheen to the leadership. But the job throws up an immense range of complexities, most of which stem from the other 10 in the team.

Parts of this England side are not functioning. Trott, out for five and 11, is no longer the pillar at No 3. Jonny Bairstow has so far fallen short of Ashes class. And Cook's own batting displays a vulnerability absent on the last tour of Australia, where he piled up 766 runs and became the second youngest after Sachin Tendulkar to pass 5,000 in Tests.

In this series Cook's bat has flashed away for 13, 50, 12, 8, 62 and 0. The two half-centuries in there are hardly negligible, but Ian Bell and Pietersen have been England's saviours. At 28, and with 25 Test centuries and 7,669 runs, Cook remains comfortably in credit. To say he was slightly embarrassed by England's escape here would be pushing it, but he did acknowledge the swing in Australia's favour.

He praised his team for 'playing some really good cricket at Lord's, fighting very hard at Trent Bridge and getting the result in this Test when we've been behind the eight ball'.

The essence of it is that England's fans have perpetually high hopes for him. He has all the classic attributes of the English icon and the individual talent to go with them. But the urn now becomes incidental.

For England to make Lord's the true measure of these sides they have to win in Durham and at the Oval (weather permitting). If retention turned out to be harder than it looked after Australia won the toss on Thursday, the lifting of that pressure ought to allow them to restate the gulf in class. Michael Clarke's men have fangs after all. They will motor to Durham nursing a grievance from this Manchester Test and knowing they fell only 15 runs short at Trent Bridge.

Squaring this series at 2-2 is not beyond them, which ought to be all the motivation Cook needs as he endeavours to impose his personality (and his bat) on an Australian side who have been allowed off the hook they swung from at Lord's. Already the winter tour becomes palpable. There will be no calming of the seas for Captain Cook.

August 6 Michael Vaughan

For all the years that Joe Root and Jonny Bairstow have been playing cricket, their foremost thought will have been to play against Australia.

Then, to do well against them. Then, to beat them. They will have wanted that winning moment, that special feeling: hitting the winning runs, taking the winning catch, being on the field when a bowler rips out an Aussie's stumps, with 25,000 people celebrating.

The feeling they will have had in Manchester on Monday is not quite deflation. They will be proud at having played in the first England team to retain the Ashes within three Tests since 1928-29. But deep down, they will also want to experience once of those moments at Durham, like 2010-11 in Sydney, 2009 and 2005 at the Oval. And that moment will come next week – if England play better than they did here.

This England team are a very honest group, and they will know that they got away with one at Old Trafford. They should have lost, and would have lost if the rain had not come. You could tell they were in two minds over whether to celebrate or not.

Alastair Cook said the right things, but he did not want to speak too loudly, because throughout this Test match, his side had been put on the back foot. England were 30 for three for the third time in the series, and there will be concern that on a pitch that carried through for the seamers and had some zest in it, they looked vulnerable. Since the start of 2012, they have only passed 400 eight times out of 44.

That tells you the batting line-up is vulnerable to any kind of movement and a good bowling attack. Australia should take that as a positive going into the series Down Under. They will be more competitive than the team we saw in 2010-11. Their target for Nov 21 in Brisbane is to prepare pitches with bounce, pace and carry.

One of the big talking points in this series has been the Decision Review System. The players have lost trust in Hot Spot. The umpires have, the crowd have, and so have we. So I would get rid of it. We are not seeing enough right decisions.

There was the Usman Khawaja controversy on the first day when no edge showed up on Hot Spot. Nor did Kevin Pietersen's on Monday, yet neither was overturned because the third umpire heard a noise.

All the talk about DRS and technology has overshadowed the fact that players have played some very average cricket shots. Khawaja played a big drive out of the rough to Graeme Swann. All right, he missed it, but it was a terrible shot. Pietersen playing a big drive to Peter Siddle, with the pressure England were under, was a poor shot.

The problem is that Ian Bell scores a great hundred at Trent Bridge, and yet we are all talking about Stuart Broad not walking. On the first day here, Michael Clarke got 125 not out, yet we all talked about the Khawaja dismissal. We have all had to speak about DRS for so long that some exceptional cricket has been overshadowed.

Australia are building towards November now. They are finding out about their group. Clarke is finding himself at No 4. He has to stay there. David Warner looks a natural at the top of the order, and it is a good idea to have left-handers up the order, so they have more right-handers facing Swann in the middle of the innings.

So I would leave the top three as it was in the second innings, with Clarke at four, Shane Watson at five and Steve Smith at six. The challenge for this inexperienced team is to go to Durham and produce another performance like they did in Manchester.

England seriously have to consider Graham Onions. He has 44 wickets at 20 this season. If he is not going to play on

Friday – on his home ground, in a back-to-back game when England would usually rest a bowler – I would be amazed if he played in the future.

Stuart Broad look like he struggled with an ankle problem, and this could be a chance to get Onions in. I would certainly be doing that. He offers them that little something: full of length, close to the stumps, making the batsman play, getting it to nibble around.

England are not doing anything here that is remarkable. They are beating the No 4 team in the world. But to get back to No 1 they are going to have to play consistently well for perhaps a year and a half. As supporters and ex-players, we should all be delighted that England have retained the Ashes.

But while Cook will be pleased that he cannot lose the urn, he will want to experience that moment, in a week's time, when they actually win it in proper fashion.

August 6 Geoffrey Boycott

Do not let anybody tell you this is the best England team of all time just because we have retained the Ashes and denied Australia the urn for the third series on the trot.

We have only played well in patches and some big players have to step up at Durham or Australia will beat us in the fourth Test.

We were lucky Australia played so badly in the first two Tests. Basically, Australia gave us a two-goal start before they turned up in Manchester.

In the first two matches their batting was awful. At Lord's their batting technique was the worst I have seen from an Australian team in 50 years of playing and commentating on cricket.

But the first time Australia made big runs and put us under pressure we buckled. Without rain yesterday I believe we would have lost.

England have some very good players but Alastair Cook, Jonathan Trott and Matt Prior are yet to make an impact. It has been left to Ian Bell, James Anderson and Graeme Swann to get us into winning positions. Our batting has not prospered. We have been in trouble a number of times in this series, at 28 for three, 30 for three, 64 for three and 37 for three. We need to address that situation if we are even going to contemplate getting back to No 1 in the world.

We are lucky we have two match-winning bowlers in Anderson and Swann. If one does not bowl the opposition out, the other does. Jimmy did at Trent Bridge and Swann took wickets here but somewhere along the line, those batsmen have got to pull their fingers out. We are not playing our best cricket. It is just that the opposition are not that good.

We are making too many basic errors as a unit. I think it is a mindset problem. They have to look to stay in. Trott is playing shots and getting out. We are always losing the top order without many runs on the board. It is an uphill struggle for others to get them out of jail. It is very difficult to make big totals when you lose early wickets.

Why do we keep saying the new ball is so crucial? Because

you have to get through it without losing wickets. It is not about how many runs you score. It is about surviving it with wickets intact. Good sides play the new ball well. Matthew Hayden and Justin Langer, Gordon Greenidge and Desmond Haynes. That is what you have to aim for.

Down the order Prior is struggling too. He was voted Player of the Year for his performances. But in seven innings since winning the award, he has averaged 17. His best innings during that time was the 31 he made in the first Test. That will not cut it for much longer. You cannot live on past performances. God help us if Bell and KP get out cheaply.

Bell has been so important, saving us with two hundreds and a 60 in the second innings here. Others have helped him but he has been the glue holding it together.

Kevin Pietersen is our one great player. He played a wonderful innings at Old Trafford. His expansive drive in the second innings when we were trying to save the game was daft. But we just have to accept that because he has that special quality.

Jonny Bairstow needs some big runs. Until he gets a hundred, he is going to have a monkey on his back. Jack Nicklaus won 18 majors but he said the hardest to win was the first one. It is the same with Jonny. He has played 11 Tests intermittently. He has been in and out of the side but when he gets a chance, he needs to make a hundred. People remember the centuries not the pretty thirties, forties or fifties. Centuries win Test matches or put you in the position to win. You can only be a promising player for so long but then you have to deliver the big runs.

Not only certain England batsmen have problems. These three Test matches have been marred by poor umpiring decisions and inconsistencies in technology. Hot Spot does not always pick up nicks: for example, when Pietersen drove away from his body in the second innings here. There was a huge noise on the stump mic, the umpire gave him out but there was nothing on Hot Spot.

In Australia's first innings, Steve Smith hit a similar big drive, and there was a huge noise on the stump mic, but the umpire gave him not out and there was nothing on Hot Spot for the third umpire to change the decision.

You cannot have a system that the players do not trust. It has to be at least 98 per cent accurate. It is supposed to help umpires get more correct decisions but it only confuses everybody, leaving players frustrated and annoyed.

Hawk-Eye is accurate. Players, commentators and the public trust it, but if we keep getting bad decisions from Hot Spot, eventually people will lose confidence in how umpires read technology. Hawk-Eye would be damaged by association, which would be a shame.

Fourth Test Durham Day One
August 10 Derek Pringle

England (238-9) v Australia

The first time Australia played at Chester-le-Street in a one-day match they were spooked by the ghosts of nearby Lumley Castle, where they stayed.

On Friday, in the first Ashes Test at the ground, England looked the more haunted side, frightened it seemed to play even the occasional shot in anger.

It was only a late rally by the tail that gave England any respectability at all, the last two wickets adding 41 runs off 56 balls to see the home team to 238 for nine at the close, after off-spinner Nathan Lyon had taken four for 42.

You would not put it past coach Darren Lehmann to dabble in exorcism for he appears to have removed the bad spirits in this Australia side and got them playing robust cricket again. Instead it was England who performed as if a hex had been put on them, their fate to drown in maidens.

Lehmann has not waved a magic wand either, just impressed on his players the need for being in the match for the long haul and for discipline with bat and ball, an approach that kept a timid England under lock and key.

Having watched Australia's travails of the first two

Investec Tests, it was natural to assume that their rally at Old Trafford was like those experienced by a stock market during recession, an unexpected blip in an otherwise depressed market.

Except that 'feel good' and 'feel bad' factors tend to last longer in sport, the ones at Old Trafford bleeding into this match without a change in the balance of power, the advantage, as there, lying with Australia.

On a slow pitch, which Alastair Cook decided was good enough to bat first on, an unchanged England allowed themselves to be dominated by a bowling attack high on discipline but low on creativity after Australia dropped the mercurial Mitchell Starc in favour of the line-and-length virtues of Jackson Bird.

Bird, in only his third Test, was given the new ball alongside Ryan Harris, though watching the almost strokeless respect he was given by Cook and Joe Root, you might have though it was the 'Big Bird' Joel Garner bowling, and he really did give nothing away. Garner's economy rate was 2.47 runs an over in his Test career, but Cook and Root did not even manage to outstrip that, only striking their first four in the 12th over.

The scoring rate sped up, relatively, once Root had been caught behind off Shane Watson and Jonathan Trott joined his captain.

Like Cook, Trott has been out of form this series, though once he had survived Australia's early attempts to get him caught down the leg side (his head has been falling over), his attempt to play himself back into it was more forceful than that of his partner's. He even struck Peter Siddle for two fours off successive balls, a curio in an otherwise dour exhibition of Test match batting.

With two men feeling for form and a pace attack determined to win the Trappist prize for discipline, a stalemate was almost reached. But Michael Clarke is a fidgety captain and while many would have been happy with the control his seam bowlers had exerted, he turned to his spinner Lyon instead.

Lyon was hit out of the attack by Kevin Pietersen at Old Trafford and was again here, thought not quite as convincingly, but not before he had dismissed Trott, caught by short leg off bat and pad trying to work the ball behind square on the on side.

Pietersen, his pride piqued by suggestions from Australia's Channel Nine that he would cheat, almost fell to Lyon first ball as he tried to dominate from the off, the miscue just dropping over mid-on's head. He later stroked him for four with a controlled drive but promptly miscued another, this time over mid-off when he was aiming over mid-on.

It was a far from convincing assault but Clarke still removed his spinner. Meanwhile, Cook reached his fifty off 152 balls, the third slowest of his career, and Pietersen moved into fifth place in the pantheon of leading England run-scorers in Tests, overtaking the 7,728 that Michael Atherton made over a 115-Test career.

With Harris sore after the previous Test and Bird still green, Lyon had to return, though this time from around the wicket, an angle that brought a hesitancy in Pietersen last seen in his travails against left-arm spin.

Whatever change the new angle brought to Pietersen's brain chemistry it was akin to him being tasered, the swaggering intent turning suddenly to wobbly defence and a thin outside edge, which saw him walk after Brad Haddin caught it.

At least Pietersen had tried to knock Australia's bowlers off their plan. Cook, by contrast, had tried to ride it out but judging from the error that led to his downfall, he had become mesmerised by his own inaction.

A misjudgment as bad as his, when he shouldered arms to a straight ball from Bird, should not happen when you have been at the crease nine minutes shy of four hours. Pressure accretes rather than dissipates when you cannot break the shackles.

Ian Bell tried to dominate after tea by going the aerial route against Lyon favoured by Pietersen. But without the same chutzpah or power as his team-mate, his miscue failed to clear mid-off where Harris took a fine running catch.

Matt Prior and Jonny Bairstow had added 34 in 19.2 overs when Siddle produced the best ball of the day, nipping one back sharply to have Prior lbw, though Australia were forced to review it after Aleem Dar gave it not out.

Bairstow followed soon after, lbw sweeping at Lyon, a decision he reviewed in vain when it was shown the ball was too straight for the shot.

Stuart Broad was then bounced out by Harris, at which point England's batsmen showed some spirit, though Australia aided Graeme Swann's sumptuous strokes by taking the second new ball, which he timed beautifully until he hooked down square leg's throat.

August 10 Jim White

We can only assume Lord Howell of Guildford is not a frequent visitor to the cricket ground at Chester-le-Street.

Looking out across the perfect symmetry of its lined outfield, beyond the swaying treeline to the castle standing sentinel up on the hillside, the cross of St George fluttering from its turrets, the last adjective that springs to mind is the one his Lordship recently used in parliament to describe the North East: 'desolate' this place is not. In fact, as the players ran round in afternoon sunshine Adelaide would be pushed to match, it could be argued this is the most picturesque setting imaginable for a cricket match. So delightful you wonder why nobody thought of playing an Ashes Test up here before.

Mind, it would have been somewhat impractical before 1992. Twenty-one years ago – and it may surprise Lord Howell to learn such things exist in this part of the world – this was open countryside. Cows were grazing where yesterday Ryan Harris was marking his run-up (and in truth, England's batsmen did their best to leave a commemorative sprinkling of manure on the wicket). Two decades on, to give the flurry of hospitality boxes and temporary stands its official title, this is now the Emirates Durham International Cricket Ground. And finally it is the scene of the biggest of all cricketing confrontations.

'It's historic is this,' said Ken Johnson, a doorman on one of the hospitality boxes. 'Last year, if you'd asked someone from Australia where Chester-le-Street was they wouldn't have had the faintest. They know now all right. It's put us right on the map has this.'

So historic is it, the local television news was describing the game as the biggest international sporting event to be staged in the North East since the Soviet Union beat Hungary in the 1966 World Cup quarter-final at Roker Park.

No wonder Durham County Cricket Club's commercial department had run up a line of T-shirts to mark the occasion and put them on sale in the club shop. For just £15 it was possible to walk round the ground telling everyone that you were there for the first Ashes Test to be played in Chester-le-Street. Just in case they had not noticed.

Not only that, the club had employed two artists in residence specifically to record this momentous episode. The painter David Downes is running up a watercolour, while the American author Benjamin Markovits is recording his impressions of the first day in an essay. Not a thriller, you imagine.

'It is important that the significance of our first Ashes Test is widely recognised and long remembered,' said Scott Sherard, Durham's commercial director. 'These newly created pieces of art and writing will be a fitting legacy, ensuring the excitement and sporting excellence live on.'

As in all things, history has been given economic meaning hereabouts. Durham County Council reckons that £20 million will be pumped into the local economy as a result of this game; not bad for a town of just 23,000 people, by far the smallest place ever to stage an Ashes Test.

Outside the ground, local entrepreneurs were doing their bit for the economic swell by flogging cricket's equivalent of those bizarre half and half scarves available at football matches. Surprising as it may seem, half and half flags, an amalgam of England's cross and Australia's stars, were shifting at a fiver a time.

In fact, so historic was the occasion, the crowd seemed cowed by the significance of it all; for much of the day, the 17,000 people packed into every available seat barely raised a song between them. True, as England scratched and stuttered, there was little for the home crowd to cheer; the sight of Jonny Bairstow and Alastair Cook doing thin impressions of Chris Tavare is enough to turn down the volume button on the barmiest of armies. But even the visiting Australia supporters marked the occasion by maintaining a respectful quiet. So tepid were things in the cheap seats that a stag party dressed in pink blouses, leather miniskirts and false moustaches left their station by the sightscreen a good hour before the close of play.

Either that or they were simply joining the ever-lengthening queue for the bar. It was only here that the new venue showed its inexperience. The beer outlets simply did not have the industrial efficiency demonstrated by more seasoned Test grounds. At Old Trafford, for instance, they flogged 400,000 pints across the five days of the recent Test. At Chester-le-Street, the fans may have been as thirsty, but the queues were enormous, snaking round crash barriers, pounds remaining in pockets far longer than in Manchester.

Still, when they finally made their way to the front of the line, the visitors will have found one thing about the new venue cosily familiar.

'Oh aye,' said one of the harassed, overworked bar staff.

'We want to make sure everyone feels at home – even those coming from down south. So we're charging them London prices.'

August 10 Scyld Berry

Famine stalks the land. Harvest-time approaches, yet England's batsmen are not making any hay. The dictum is to wait until both sides have had their first innings before passing judgment. But after such a disastrous first day, it can be said that England will need Graeme Swann more than ever if they are to stop Australia rallying to 2-1 down – and boosting their confidence for this winter immeasurably.

With one Test to go, this is the first summer of this millennium in which England have not amassed a total of 400. Their highest, and best, total to date came in the second innings at Trent Bridge when they had to overturn a first innings deficit of 65, and went on to score 375 – sufficient for that 13-run victory.

The last time England went through a summer without scoring 400 was in 1999, when English cricket was at its all-time most chaotic – and when only four home Tests were played because of the World Cup.

Since then, this statistic has been an accurate indicator of England's strength. As Duncan Fletcher's reign as coach, and Michael Vaughan's as captain, reached fulfilment, England passed 400 at least five times a summer from 2002 to 2006; and they did so again in 2011 when they went to No 1 in the world Test rankings.

Drought often plays a part in famines, and this summer has not been an exception. The unnaturally dry pitches which England have ordered for this summer's Tests, against Australia and New Zealand, and which have been designed for Swann primarily and England's reverse-swingers, have made unfamiliar hunting grounds for England's batsmen.

The ends can be said to have justified the means, until now: England have not lost any of those Tests, and totals of 300 have been good enough to defeat Australia and wallop New Zealand. But such low horizons will have to be raised in Australia this winter.

Lower totals than normal for an English summer are also the consequence of having a new opening pair. Nobody could expect Alastair Cook and Joe Root to replicate Hobbs and Sutcliffe after one practice game against Essex in which to get to know each other.

Individually, Cook may be on the downward spiral, which has afflicted the run-making output of all recent England captains following an initial surge on appointment. Root has scored only 78 runs apart from his 180 at Lord's, although he has batted a long time: only Ian Bell, on either side, has faced more balls.

Throw in Jonathan Trott's bad trot and the result was a poor start by England in every innings of the second and third Tests. But this did not apply on Friday: England's batsmen had made a decent start before they decided to impose themselves on Nathan Lyon, and failed.

The sustained accuracy of Shane Watson, and of

Australia's pace bowlers in general, should not be over-looked. Watson has acted like a boa constrictor: he may have swallowed only two victims but he has tied England down to 1.8 runs an over.

In series of three Tests or more over the past decade, Jacques Kallis is the only other seamer to have an economy rate below two an over. Another factor in England's failure to amass a large total on Friday may have been selflessness. It sounds absurd that hardened pros could be accused of such a trait, but trends in cricket can swing like pendulums.

A generation ago for instance, at every level, a young leg-spinner would not be given any chance; now he may open the bowling in a 20-over game, given too much of a chance.

Similarly, an England Test batsman of a generation ago was shooting himself in the foot if he did a selfless act. No allowance would be made, no credit given. The rule was to look after number one up until 1999, the year of maximum chaos, before central contracts were introduced.

Was England's strategy yesterday to go after Lyon and hit him out of the attack? It was at Old Trafford: Kevin Pietersen and Bell launched into Lyon and took him for 29 from four overs, before he could maul England.

Here England's right-handed batsmen perished in the cause of attacking Lyon. Impatient? Yes. Imprudent? Yes, given a turning pitch where it is imperative to score first-innings runs before batting becomes ever harder. Selfish? No.

Day Two
August 11 Scyld Berry

Australia (222-5) trail England (238) by 16 runs

It could have been Headingley, back in the day when men were men, and fish and chips cost sixpence. The Riverside was covered by cloud the entire day and the ball jagged all over the shop, especially when new, to make batting as difficult as it had been in Leeds when the pitch was notoriously fickle. Batting was much harder than on the opening day in other words, and yet Australia had reached 222 for five by the time that bad light stopped play.

A lead of three figures on Sunday would come close to guaranteeing victory for Australia, so capricious is this pitch becoming, and then at the Oval the Investec series would be all too alive so far as England are concerned.

Since Lord's the pendulum has been steadily shifting in the tourists' favour and the pieces of their jigsaw are fitting into place. Chris Rogers, by making his maiden Test century in the most arduous circumstances, has filled one problem position, and so has Shane Watson at No 6, as a batting allrounder.

Together Rogers and Watson shared a stand of 129 that took Australia to within touching distance of England's 238 – or spitting distance might be a more appropriate term, after England's advantage in winning the toss had been so wasted. Had the last two sessions been played out at Old Trafford a week ago, England would not have survived in their present batting form.

If Australia take a lead of any note on Sunday, the pressure on England's batsmen in their second innings will be telling – telling us, specifically, how their careers are progressing or otherwise. This is the beauty and cruelty of the five-Test series: there is no hiding-place for a player to flounder ashore, as in a three-Test series.

The batting of Jonny Bairstow and Matt Prior are two major concerns. Bairstow in his second innings has to show that he can find other scoring options against Australia's pace bowlers. In his first innings it was as if Bairstow's air supply had been cut off when Michael Clarke placed not only a mid-on but a very straight short mid-on.

Prior has been well and truly Siddled. Four times in this series, and nine in all, Peter Siddle has dismissed him. The motor in England's engine-room is stuttering. Prior's opposite number, Brad Haddin, resumes this morning with a series aggregate of 171 runs to Prior's 86, although Prior had the pleasure of his 200th Test catch on Saturday.

Rogers at least has shown England's batsmen how to bat on this pitch, by playing very late with a reduced backlift and a lot of luck. The veteran novice – a novice in his fifth Test, yet a veteran with 60 first-class centuries before Saturday – must be glad now that he did not make his maiden Test hundred on what was a belter at Old Trafford. His work here has been up with the best of his illustrious predecessors, Matthew Hayden and Justin Langer.

Rogers' luck came in the form of a couple of inside-edges past his stumps; a review being overturned after Tony Hill had given him caught behind when 22; and being dropped by Graeme Swann low to his right at second slip when 49.

One of those 'Chinese cuts' vividly illustrated the latent devil in this pitch: the ball from Stuart Broad that darted back and lifted so steeply that Rogers had to leap to keep it down. It was not only England's bowlers who made the ball talk. Jackson Bird did so when finishing off England's innings without addition to their 238 for nine.

For both sides the new ball swung; but there was even more lateral movement when Broad pitched a full length and made the ball seam sharply off the loose surface of yet another over-dry pitch. The over-dryness of this pitch is even more questionable than in previous Tests of this series, because the rest of the Riverside is bright green. A pitch should not be completely different from the rest of a square, for then nature has not been allowed to play its part.

Broad took his first three wickets in his opening spell of seven overs, and the fourth just before the premature close. Yet he might not have played at all, or at least he might not have been given the new ball, if Graham Onions had been selected – a cry that went up as Australia rallied from 76 for four.

David Warner was trapped on his crease by Broad, while Usman Khawaja was undecided about whether to play or leave. Clarke, tied down, played a drive that was more of a hack and was caught high up at first slip by his counterpart.

If this had been Trent Bridge or Lord's, Australia could have been expected to collapse. But not here. The youthful inconsistency is being ironed out of a young side, largely because Rogers has secured one end in the third and fourth Tests, and made all the difference.

Watson seemed calmer for Rogers' influence. Instead of going hard at the ball as he had as an opener, he waited patiently for it to come to him. He worked his way through the 20s and 30s that have been so perilous, and only then turned on the blistering drive that is his hallmark, nearly taking one of James Anderson's feet with it.

If Cook missed a trick, it was in not bowling Swann more at Rogers. On reaching 96, Rogers started to bat more like a three-year-old than a 35-year-old against Swann, such was his desire to consummate his life's ambition. But he swept across the line, and was not bowled, but fulfilled.

August 11 Steve James

One for the oldies. Chris Rogers scored his maiden Test century at the age of 35 on Saturday, and it was a wonderfully heart-warming triumph for persistence and hope.

It was his 61st first-class hundred – and his most worthy – but it was surely his hardest. For 19 long balls he was stuck on 96, as the magnitude of his nearing achievement dawned, and Graeme Swann probed at his nerves like a dentist. Twice Rogers nearly chipped the ball to fielders on the leg side. Once he tried to cut a ball that was nowhere near short or wide enough for the purpose.

But then he swept hard at Swann. There might even have been a hint of desperation. The suffering had gone on for too long.

The contact was firm and, with no man back in the deep, the ball sped to the deep square-leg boundary. He had done it. But you would have never known initially.

Rogers simply jogged to the non-striker's end and back to the middle of the pitch to meet his partner Brad Haddin. There was no fist-pumping or leaping in the air, as the modern peacocks do. He removed his helmet and raised his bat in the air.

It was the most old-fashioned of celebrations from a very old-fashioned and, in modern cricketing terms, a very old Test cricketer. Rogers will be 36 at the end of the month.

He had played just one Test before this tour, miserly reward for over 20,000 first-class runs at an average of over 50. Circumstance had meant that he was a victim of Australia's golden generation. Matthew Hayden and Justin Langer were a rather useful opening partnership, after all.

But the truth is that Langer could not have played any better than Rogers did on Saturday. He would have scrapped away, just as Rogers did. He would have watched the ball like a hawk, playing it as late as he could, just as Rogers did. He would have played and missed, and then forgot it ever happened, just as Rogers did.

The comparison is rather ironic because when Rogers left Western Australia for Victoria in 2008 there were rumours that there had been a rift between the two. More likely was a fall-out with coach Tom Moody, but Rogers and Langer were never close then, their attitudes rather different. But then few can match Langer's relentlessly intense work ethic. Few ever will.

It is said that there is much mutual respect between the pair these days, as Rogers mentioned Langer's motto 'you've just got to fight as hard as you can' after Australia's limp batting display at Lord's, and that will only be increased after this. For this truly was a fight. Rogers was gutsiness personified. The pitch was tricky, with Stuart Broad bowling a couple of magnificent spells.

It was like the early years of Durham's first-class career when batsmen usually retreated from here with broken digits, bruised feet and dented pride. But for all the movement, it always seemed that, if you could develop a partnership, things would become easier. And that's what Rogers and Shane Watson did during the afternoon in a partnership of 129. It did become easier and it could just be the partnership that decides the match.

Australia made many mistakes before this series began, but selecting Rogers was most certainly not one of them. They had gone back to their previous strengths in picking tough, battle-hardened cricketers. Just imagine if they had also kept Mike Hussey for a little longer, rather than looking wishfully to youth. The Ashes might have been in jeopardy, and not just this match.

August 11 Jim White

There was a spell of three balls just before lunch on Saturday which, if anyone is compiling a record of Stuart Broad's career, would serve as definitive evidence of him at his very best. He was bowling against Chris Rogers and the

Australian limpet was struggling. As the ball cut away from his bat viciously from a length, Rogers was twice left wafting at the air, unable to judge flight, trajectory or movement. The third ball, threatening to perform on-field surgery, almost cut him in half.

As Rogers ducked in the attempt to avoid having his kidneys forcibly removed, the ball snicked the outside of his bat and shot towards the boundary. There was only one reaction that was appropriate: Rogers exchanged knowing grins with Broad. Everything was written in those smiles. At that moment, the two of them – tormentor and victim – knew precisely who was in charge.

That morning spell was Broad at his very best. It was one of those sessions in which he made every ball a drama. He took three wickets and would have had a fourth – Rogers himself – had the decision been left to the umpire and not the machinations of the referral system.

Seven overs, three maidens, three wickets for 20 runs was Broad's morning work. But those figures indicated little of his excellence. The number of times he beat the bat, with a tad more good fortune he might have wrapped up the innings before anyone had a chance to engage with the Durham catering. The Aussies looked as bemused by what was going on as a punch-drunk kangaroo.

He is an oddly unpredictable cricketer, Stuart Broad. For much of this series he has looked what an Australian would term 'ordinary'. Until Saturday, his Ashes appeared as though they would largely be remembered for his refusal to walk at Trent Bridge. And then, just as a swell of innuendo about his place in the England side was beginning to develop, he produced a performance of unequivocal excellence.

It is a pattern that has marked his working practice throughout his time as a Test player. Not for Broad cosy consistency. His career has more peaks and troughs than an Alpine skier. But what peaks they are: six for 91 in an innings at Headingley in the 2009 Ashes, seven for 72 against West Indies at Lord's in 2012, seven for 44 against New Zealand at Lord's in 2013.

Those who have watched him closely say the story is written in his bowling action. This is not the insistent metronome of Glenn McGrath. His left ankle bends under him in the delivery stride, meaning his body falls away rather than smoothly following through. Uncertain whether it will produce a short, good length or over-pitched delivery, his action is not something to instil confidence.

But when he is feeling good, when assurance is generated from other sources – his batting, for instance – the deficiencies in his technique are negated. He looks devastating.

Saturday morning he was way too sharp for this Australia. David Warner was the first to discover quite how good he was, bowled by a ball that he clearly did not see. Then Usman Khawaja, so confused he managed to both leave and play at the same time, edged to Matt Prior, before the captain Michael Clarke sliced an extravagant drive to Alistair Cook.

If the DRS system had disentangled itself sufficiently to give Rogers out when Broad was convinced he had edged a ball that in fact had trapped him lbw, Australia would have been buried.

It was just as well Broad was bowling like that. At the other end, James Anderson was singularly failing to make the most of cloudy conditions apparently tailor-made for his swing. Tim Bresnan looked no more than steady. But Broad's ability to land the ball on its seam was beautifully exploited.

Or at least it was until lunch. After that Rogers and Shane Watson seized the initiative with a belligerent demonstration of old-fashioned Aussie cussedness. Broad, by now requiring careful husbanding to ensure the one functioning bit of England's armoury was not exhausted by overuse, was obliged to watch from mid-on as a surfeit of stubbornness overwhelmed England's efforts.

But then Cook, with more than a hint of desperation, realised he had to unleash his one functioning threat before bad light undermined his strategy. And the threat duly delivered, immediately dismissing Watson on his return. Nothing else could have been expected: it was the perfect reminder that this was, after all, Broad's day.

August 11 Geoffrey Boycott

This summer England have not made 400 runs once in an innings. That tells you how poor our batting has been and how pathetic Australia's has been at times to have not beaten us.

England's bowlers have got them out of jail so many times but it is time we started batting well. You cannot improve on anything unless you are prepared to put your hand up and admit your mistakes. That is the first priority. Our top three batsmen – Alastair Cook, Joe Root and Jonathan Trott – have not been in good form in this series.

I congratulate the efforts of Trott and Cook on Friday, because they are both out of nick and yet they grafted hard for their runs. Top-class players make hard-working, ugly fifties when not in form, because that helps the side and themselves so credit to them for showing mental tenacity and great character.

But some of the others leave me shaking my head in disbelief. Root is a young kid with enormous talent learning his trade. He likes to stay back to the seam bowlers. There is nothing wrong with that as an opener.

The bowlers are quicker and you do not want to commit yourself forward in case they bowl you a short ball. But when they pitch it up you need to be able to transfer your weight and make a big stride forward to get near the pitch of the ball.

He is getting caught on the crease. He is neither forward nor back. He is in no-man's-land, which means from when the ball pitches to when he plays it, it has much further to travel. If it moves off the pitch he is a candidate for nicking it to slip or the keeper. The idea is to get as near to the pitch of the ball as you can to reduce the distance it travels and can move.

This was always my concern about him moving from the middle order to opening. When people say, 'Hang on, he opens the batting for Yorkshire,' I would argue that he does, but the bowling in international cricket is much better and usually a bit quicker. Therefore it exposes any weaknesses.

For the moment he has lost the immaculate footwork he showed against New Zealand. It is footwork that makes batting. He has regressed. It is liable to happen with young kids. I do not know any 22-year-old who is the finished article.

We can all have precocious talent but we have to learn, gain experience and mature. He will be fine, trust me. I am a huge supporter. But the road to the top is not straightforward. I know he made 180 at Lord's. It was a wonderful innings. But if he had been caught on eight when the keeper did not move for it, his scores in this series would be 8, 13, 6, 8, 30 and 5. It does not look too clever without the 180.

Kevin Pietersen came out firing. He was probably hot under the collar because of the fuss about Hot Spot. I, too, would have been bloody cross if they had inferred that I was cheating. But he played the non-spinning off-spinner with half a bat running it to third man. It was naive. You should hit the ball back from whence it came. The angle is around the wicket, wide on the crease so hit it back to mid-on or to the bowler. It is the safest shot in the book.

Then Ian Bell played the worst shot of the whole innings. Here is one of our top batsmen in the form of his life. The team was in trouble. They needed him to stick around in the final session. But what did he do? He had sat on his bum having a cuppa and a cream cake during the tea interval.

But four balls after the interval he tried to smack the off-spinner over the top. It was a recipe for disaster. He is probably so confident and full of himself he thought, 'I have got runs, I can do anything and I won't get dropped.' I am telling you if he had played that shot at Yorkshire in the

1960s when Brian Close was captain he might have got a bunch of fives for it. It was a thoughtless act.

Jonny Bairstow hung on while Australia were strangling the innings, bowling maidens and waiting for the new ball. Having nearly got through that with three overs to the new ball he tried to sweep the off-spinner pitching on middle stump.

To compound it he even reviewed the decision when it was knocking middle stump out of the ground. You have to think better than that at this level. It is not just about talent. It is about using your brain.

We have to start doing better than this. We cannot go on hoping the bowlers will get us out of trouble or the opposition bat poorly. How many times have I said that when you bat well, you control the game?

Our bowlers will win matches, but it should not be an uphill struggle for them all the time to get the batsmen out of a big mess.

Day Three
August 12 Derek Pringle

England (238 & 234-5) lead Australia (270) by 202 runs

Ian Bell has played the lead role several times already in this Investec Ashes series but he appears to have acquired a taste for inhabiting the limelight after scoring his third hundred of the series.

Only three men have now made three hundreds for England in home Ashes series – Bell, David Gower in 1985 and Maurice Leyland in 1934. While the first two share grace of stroke and an air of insouciance Leyland was more like Chris Rogers. Mind you, Bell had a Rogers moment on 97 when he almost edged Jackson Bird to Michael Clarke at first slip, the ball just clearing Australia's captain.

Bell's century, with power to add today, was arguably his best of the series given the pressure he found himself under when he joined Kevin Pietersen at the crease with the score on 49 for three.

With a deficit of 32 runs on first innings, England were just 17 runs ahead at that stage and in danger of placing their 2-0 lead under serious duress had they collapsed further. The urn might be safe but the series has yet to be secured, though that should be a formality if Bell bats until lunch today after England closed on 233 for five, a lead of 201 runs.

Few players relish tense situations but Bell and Pietersen, through current form and reputation, were made for it. Shane Warne has a theory that Bell is more confident batting with a dominant batsman such as Pietersen though his thoughts on the matter did not suggest the alpha male would be outplayed to the extent he was here yesterday.

Pietersen began sensibly though with positive intent, like most of England's top order, following their inert batting in the first innings. Yet, Bell was in another dimension altogether, the crisp timing of his drives and canny placement of his cuts prising free the grip Australia have enjoyed since the opening session.

He soon overtook Pietersen who never quite matched his fluency on a pitch where the sting in the lateral plane, if not the horizontal, had begun to subside. Their partnership of 106 in 33 overs made their team's prospects of winning this match flip-flop to the good in just over two hours.

Even Pietersen's dismissal to Nathan Lyon for 44, after he skewed a leading edge to Chris Rogers at extra cover, gave England little pause for thought, such was the power of Bell's innings. Indeed, Jonny Bairstow batted as Pietersen might have done had he reached his fifty, boldly with some savage striking, especially off Lyon.

Nobody can be sure what a secure total on the fifth day here is, as no match here has ever experienced play on all five days. Two Tests against the West Indies here have been last-day finishes, but in both games, a day had been washed out, so the pitch's behaviour over a five-stretch is not known.

Earlier this season Yorkshire successfully chased 336 here for six wickets down, Joe Root making 182. He did not look like making a fraction of that here this time after being bowled by Ryan Harris, but he can offer helpful pointers to his captain should England find themselves in a position to declare later today.

Alastair Cook will err on the side of caution if he has that luxury. As in Manchester, the captain only has to draw the match rather than win it to take the series, so he may just wait until his team are bowled out.

He set the tone yesterday, batting with more purpose yesterday than the first time around. Although Root still looked too timid, after Australia's pace bowlers drew him onto a front foot he seems increasingly reluctant to use, Cook was busy. Yet just as Michael Clarke had done in the first innings he undid the good work with a rash shot, edging Harris behind as he tried to drive on the up through the covers.

Jonathan Trott played in similar vein, almost springing the leg-side trap no Australian captain has bothered to set in an Ashes Test since they snared David Gower that way 23 years ago. But just as they appeared to have exhausted that particular line of inquiry, Harris produced a snorting bouncer which he gloved to Haddin.

At that point Bell and Pietersen took charge, though both men's prosperity required the odd slice of good fortune. Pietersen inside-edged Lyon close to his stumps while Bell, on 37, saw an inside edge off Harris narrowly elude Haddin's gloves.

Harris was immense in carrying Australia's attack. A stocky bowler in the mould of Rodney Hogg who is a big fan, he is direct and hits the pitch hard without compromising his control. His problem is that he rarely stays fit long enough to get a run in the side. Had he done so, Australia's self-belief, rock bottom at the start of this series, would have surely been restored before now.

Clarke's team began the day with the opportunity to bury England, or at least put them deep in the mire. Rogers had battled his way to a maiden Test hundred the previous day and was hungry for more while Haddin's pugnacity is known to get results. They also had 32 balls to settle before the second new ball was due, a period neither man survived after Graeme Swann dismissed both in the space of nine balls.

With the score 236 for seven, James Anderson and Stuart Broad took the second new ball on cue, though it did not prove as lethal as most had predicted and Harris was able to belt five fours in his quick-fire 28. Eventually, he was last man out lbw to Broad, the fast bowler's fifth wicket, but only after Anderson had dismissed Siddle and Lyon.

England needed to ask for a review to get Harris, after umpire Tony Hill had declined their appeal. When TV replays appeared on the big screen it was so obviously out that there was the unprecedented sight of Harris walking off before the TV umpire had conveyed his thoughts to Hill. For that, Harris could be found guilty of dissent, yet why waste valuable time if you know the end is nigh?

August 12 Simon Hughes

Bell disturbed Australians all day in Durham on Sunday. The chimes began from the great tower of the cathedral at 8am, and continued all morning, calling worshippers to a succession of services, waking those travelling supporters who had over-indulged on Durham hospitality the night before.

By the time the cathedral clock struck 12 England's Bell had his pads on and was ready to deliver his sermon. Thou shalt not get past my straight bat was his first commandment and he practised what he preached for most of the afternoon. He was still in residence by the time the ringers were summoning the faithful to Evensong.

It was an immaculate performance. There were no flowery shots, or flirty wafts, or incomprehensible dances up the pitch to lob the ball to mid-off. The defence was impregnable, the footwork certain, the bat swing controlled. He recognised that playing casually across the line of straight balls or driving on the up were shots loaded with risk, so he cut them out of his game.

The Durham pitch is not difficult but it is capricious. It plays sly tricks on lazy or overambitious shots. After Joe Root had been bowled by an absolute peach from Ryan Harris, Alastair Cook drove loosely and was caught behind, and Jonathan Trott flapped at a well-directed bouncer which flicked his glove. England at that point led by just 17 runs.

Some time ago Bell shed the reputation as someone who scores hundreds only after others have done so, but a feature of this series is that he has made runs when England have really needed them. At Trent Bridge they were only a few in front in their second innings when he came to the wicket, and at Lord's England were 28 for three when he walked in. In each case he converted a shaky position into one of considerable strength. He did the same on Sunday.

He has struck a superb balance between resilience and resourcefulness. He has perfectly embraced a batsman's twin aims – to stay in but also to make runs. It sounds obvious but England lurched from stationary to free-wheeling in their first innings. Initially Bell looked to score mainly on the back foot, understanding that the pitch's slowness made driving dangerous.

He pulled a two and dabbed a four through the slip cordon, beautifully riding the bounce. He went up on his toes and caressed a short ball from Jackson Bird through point for four. Only when the ball was genuinely over-pitched and straight did he dare to drive.

He was careful in defence. The flex in his knees when the ball stayed low, the flexibility in his body and arms when the ball lifted unpredictably, kept his precious wicket intact. He would not be drawn into an airy swish outside off stump. He left the ball judiciously. He gave no chance. He withstood a bumper barrage from Harris towards the end, smiling when a snorter put him on his backside, the expression disguising a hardening of his determination.

The regal strokes – the delicious off drive, the deft late cut – were only unfurled when it was safe to do so, but he was as fluent as the conditions would allow. He outscored Kevin Pietersen in their stand of 106.

Bell has delivered on the team mantra: don't leave it to someone else. He has shouldered the responsibility of elevating the innings out of the doldrums and only exited the scene when the job was done. Significantly England have never lost a Test when Bell has made a hundred. And, barring a miracle, they are not going to lose this one. The Australians' only option is to answer the call to prayers in the morning. The problem is if God were a cricketer, he would bat like Ian Bell.

August 12 Jim White

Despite turning up late in the Old Trafford gloaming last week, the England cricket team insist they pay no heed to weather forecasts. There must have been an explanation, then, beyond the threatening front skidding across meteorologists' charts in the direction of Chester-le-Street, for Alastair Cook's skittish cameo of an innings on Sunday.

Rather than trying to finish things long before the clouds intervened, he must have been doing something else. Like trying to hit himself back into form. This has been an odd series for Cook. The satisfaction of retaining the urn in his first Ashes encounter as England captain will have been tempered by concerns about his own contribution. Sure, his bucket-like hands have been in full working order in the slip cordon.

True, he is ahead of his counterpart Michael Clarke in the use of the Decision Review System (and how he needed to be on Sunday when the unerring eye of technology helpfully negated the doddery incompetence of the onfield umpires). But Cook is a man who defines himself by his batting. And so far in this series, his batting has been well short of the dazzling peak it attained in his early days as captain.

On Sunday what we saw was a fine batsman struggling to make sense of his dip in form. In the first innings here in Durham, he had been scratching and scrabbling around without point or purpose. When Geoffrey Boycott criticises you for being unnecessarily pedestrian, then you know you have a problem.

So when he walked out with Joe Root after Australia had been efficiently dispatched in the morning session, he appeared determined to put such negativity behind him. Like a golfer who had remodelled his swing overnight, he came out with a new modus operandi. In his first over he clipped a ball from Ryan Harris off his pads to the boundary; in the next he squirted one from Jackson Bird through the slip cordon.

It was an aggressive signal of intent. His aggression sent a message back to the dressing room: there can be no hanging around if this Test is to be won. The trouble was, his form has dipped sufficiently to undermine such a radical departure from his standard approach. He was trying to accelerate but velocity is limited when the ball refuses to find the middle of the bat. Try as he might, no one could accuse him of bullying the opposition.

Day Four

August 13 Derek Pringle

England (238 & 330) beat Australia (270 & 224) by 74 runs

The grouse might disagree but the Glorious 12th at least lived up to billing for Stuart Broad and England, after the fast bowler bagged six wickets to clinch both the match and the series for his team.

Shooting parties can create a lot of carnage in a couple of hours on the moors at this time of year, but they would do well to outdo the mayhem Broad inflicted on Australia in 45 balls at Chester-le-Street when he took six for 20. One minute David Warner was set to land a bigger blow on England than he did on Joe Root, the next he and the top order were back in the coop, their hopes of chasing 299 for victory highly realistic at 168 for two, crushed by an irresistible spell of fast bowling.

Broad's heroics in this Test, which amounted to 11 for 121 and the best match figures of his career, mean that England have now won the last three Ashes series. Such a sequence was last managed in 1981 albeit with a centenary Test and a series post-Kerry Packer in which the Ashes were not disputed in the mix. Before that such dominance had not occurred since 1956, of which only a handful of combatants remain alive.

Until Broad intervened, such a victory looked likely to be delayed until the Oval after Australia began their pursuit nervelessly through Warner and Chris Rogers, the pair adding 109 for the first wicket. But Broad has always been prone to hot streaks and having done it once against Australia in a crucial game at the Oval in 2009, where his intelligent use of cutters and a debut hundred by Jonathan Trott helped to clinch the series, a reprise was never out of the question once he had got the sequence under way with the wicket of Michael Clarke.

Until he began to add aggression to the reverse swing, which had begun to happen around the 40-over mark, England's prospects had looked bleak. Although Tim Bresnan had taken the crucial wicket of Warner, who made a fine 71, it was Broad that discombobulated Australia's hopes when he bowled Clarke, the captain, with the first ball after drinks.

It was a ball to rival the pearl that James Anderson dismissed Clarke with at Trent Bridge, though he did play it on the walk as he has done against the reverse-swinging ball ever since it first confounded him in 2005. With their captain gone, Broad and Bresnan removed the next four in the order for seven runs in 28 balls as Australia froze in the face of a seemingly unstoppable force.

Thereafter, it was only a race against time and bad light, the extra half an hour allowed by the umpires but then compromised when the light dimmed and Cook was forced to use spinners at each end. For those wanting to witness the dispatch by the close, which was not Durham CCC, given the 5,500 tickets they had sold for Tuesday, the sun came out on cue for Broad to return and take the final wicket, Peter Siddle caught at mid-off.

It would be easy to say this was a classic case of a side used to winning overcoming one used to losing, though you would have struggled to identify which team was which at tea when Australia were 120 for one in their second innings after 33 overs. Having seen the ball bounce erratically when they batted, especially when Australia took the second new ball, England would have been confident of making quick inroads into Australia's second innings.

It did not happen that way and while ball beat bat on occasion, neither Anderson nor Broad looked as dangerous, initially, as Ryan Harris had earlier after the barrel-chested opening bowler had taken a Test best seven for 117.

It was not long before nervous glances were being exchanged as Warner and Rogers, the yin and yang of south-paw batsmen, eased past the 50 mark on a fourth-day pitch that should have been making life difficult for them.

There was only one thing for Cook to do, resort to Swann,

that scourge of left-handers everywhere let alone on a pitch pitted with foot-holes outside their off stump. But Warner has blind spots when it comes to decorum in Birmingham bars let alone the etiquette of playing off-spinners on wearing pitches and he dispensed with any niceties by immediately striking Swann for six over extra cover.

It was an incredible shot and you could see the postures of England's players tighten as the partnership passed 100. But Swann turned one to have Rogers caught at slip just before tea and when Usman Khawaja was lbw to the same bowler soon after the break, they only needed Warner for belief to be restored.

It came too, though it needed a beauty from Bresnan, his fourth ball after Cook had switched him to the Finchale end. Batsmen as short as Warner are difficult to find a length to and England were either too full or too short, until Bresnan managed to land one between the two that then had enough extra bounce to find the edge.

Bresnan managed one more wicket, when he had Shane Watson lbw whipping across and inswinger, but that apart it was all Broad as Australia's batting frailties were once more exposed in the face of his ruthless precision with the moving ball.

Such an outcome had not looked so certain when the day's play began. England would have liked to bat Australia out of sight but they needed Ian Bell, their champion of the series, to see off the second new ball for that to happen, something he did not accomplish after adding just eight runs to his overnight score.

Unsurprisingly, given his excellence in the last two matches, it was Harris who produced the ball to remove Bell, a grubber that kept low and which Bell diverted onto the stumps off the inside edge of his bat.

It was a ball open to interpretations, especially when it was followed by one that bounced alarmingly to strike Matt Prior on his elbow before also diverting onto the stumps to put Harris, who finished the innings with seven for 117, on a hat-trick.

Broad prevented it but the propaganda had been sown, at least in England's minds, that this was a pitch Australia would be lucky to reach 150 on, and the remaining batsmen threw the bat confident that they probably had enough.

Indeed, that confidence worked in their favour as Bresnan and Swann added 42 runs at a run a ball for the ninth wicket, Bresnan's unbeaten 45 arguably his finest innings for England. Later, when they bowled, that certainty seemed misplaced until Broad combined aggression and reverse swing. Only then did it look as if their plan had been under control all along.

August 13 Michael Vaughan

Over the last two days of this match England have played the brand of cricket I want to see them produce 90 per cent of the time. When in trouble they have been bold and come out fighting. On Sunday morning Australia were 16 runs behind with five wickets in the tank. But England realised this was their moment and raced through the gears.

Graeme Swann took two wickets before the new ball and

England restricted them to a lead of 32. You could sense a real togetherness. Then Alastair Cook, a man out of form, attacked. Ian Bell produced another marvellous innings and Tim Bresnan sensed he had to go on the offensive yesterday morning when wickets fell.

They were also calm in the field when Australia got their chase off to a great start. I did not see any panic. They must have been worrying inside but they gave off a calm vibe. I liked the way Cook moved his fielders. He worked out where David Warner and Chris Rogers were going and he spread the field but kept two catchers in play.

His best move was his decision to replace Swann with Bresnan even though his spinner had taken two wickets. He noticed the ball had started swinging just a touch. It was one of those moments when you knew England had to go for it.

They took the big wicket of Warner and from nowhere Stuart Broad produced a great spell, up there with the best produced by Ian Botham, Bob Willis and Andrew Flintoff. He bowled 91 mph and that kind of pace just shows he is the sort of player you want in your team. He has an inner hunger and wants to come out and do something special when the team needs it.

Also credit to England for looking after the ball so well. We did not have reverse-swinging conditions. The ground was lush and it had been raining. But I could see Anderson working on it to keep it dry so it would reverse. That was one small difference between the two sides. Australia did not reverse it once during the Test.

I feel for Ian Bell. He has now scored three hundreds in

the series without winning the man-of-the-match award. He is in a league of his own, a real pleasure to watch. That inner calm and strength he has when in form is combined with a technique good enough to get him out of trouble when he misjudges line or length.

He has waited for so long to be the Mr Dependable in the side. He was frustrated when people said he could not produce under pressure. But he has found a way and it is a joy to watch when he comes in. He reminds me of Sri Lanka's Mahela Jayawardene. You know he will walk in and get his team out of trouble.

The two Yorkie lads, Joe Root and Jonny Bairstow, who are both struggling, should go and spend some time with Bell learning his methods and techniques. He has been there himself. He knows what it feels like to be under pressure. Joe should copy what Bell does with his front foot. He gets it flat, so he can move it again. That is what Joe needs, more balance on his front foot.

As for Australia, this will really hurt them. They have forgotten how to win. They will say they were robbed by rain at Old Trafford, but they did not win and have lost seven out of eight Tests.

They have forgotten how to get over the line. To lose by 74 runs, chasing 299 when they were 147 for one is some collapse.

The likes of Shane Watson, Usman Khawaja and Steve Smith got out in ways that will have been very disappointing for Darren Lehmann. I believe we will see lot of personnel changes in their batting order for the winter.

For a player of his ability it is just plain dumb for Watson to continue playing across his front pad. England set the field. It is obvious what is going on so stay leg side and hit it through the off side. To go across the stumps and work it to where the fielders are does not make sense. I have to question his brains to be a top player. I would rather see him caught or bowled than get those pads in the way again.

Khawaja fell lbw to a straight ball from Swann. He got his bat stuck but that kind of dismissal should not be happening to an Australian No 3. It was a soft dismissal.

England will win at the Oval. I would be amazed if it does not end 4-0. Australia had something to play for in this match. A 2-2 draw in the series was a carrot for them and they felt they could take it. At tea they would have been cock a hoop. It was in the bag. But now they go to the Oval with nothing to play for. They will be so flat knowing they should have won this game.

August 13 Scyld Berry

Stuart Broad is a big game hunter. Not only is he big, and game, and a hunter, he also hunts big game – and it was the wicket of Australia's captain, Michael Clarke, that brought out the best and most predatory bowling of Broad's career to consummate England's summer.

Clarke is the batsman that Broad has dismissed most often, along with the South African AB de Villiers, almost as illustrious. Of the 212 Test wickets he has taken, at 30 runs each, Broad has dismissed Clarke seven times.

To hunt down his prime target, Broad had switched to

the Lumley Castle end to have the benefit of the strong cross wind, as he said after sealing this series. In Broad's first over after the drinks break, when Australia were still on course, he produced the perfect ball: it shaped away past Clarke's bat and hit the top of off stump.

Clarke's broken wicket was a sight to inflame the hunter. Having bagged the leader of the herd, Broad ran amok and put the rest of the herd to flight, dragging his victims down one by one.

In the morning Broad had been given a vicious bouncer by Ryan Harris that he had fended from his face. He dished out a few bouncers in return, but mainly he hit a length fuller than his norm and maximised the seam movement at his fastest pace.

Broad has been on a roll before, but this was still a gripping spectacle for its ruthlessness. The Australians had nowhere to hide as Broad picked them off, registering his best Test figures of 11 for 121. He had done it before against Australia. He had been blooded as a Test bowler at the Oval in 2009 when Australia took lunch at 61 for no wicket. By tea they were 133 for eight and shot to pieces, Broad having taken the lion's share of five wickets for 37.

Everything has to come together for Broad to have one of these fits of passion. At Trent Bridge, in a similar situation, when Australia required 311 rather than 299, he had not risen to the occasion: his right shoulder was hurting and he was short of confidence.

In the first three Tests of this series he had not fired: only six expensive wickets. But when the hour came, and his country needed him, he rose to this occasion – and the damage he did should have a far-reaching effect.

Losing nine wickets in a session will be a scar that this Australian side take into the return series this winter, and maybe one or two players will never recover. Usman Khawaja will be roasted for the limp defensive prod that he aimed at Swann when Australia were 147 for one. He could well be replaced in the Oval Test by Phil Hughes and Australia's experiment with their Asian immigrant population will be shelved.

Steve Smith gloved a bouncer from Broad down into his stumps. He had earlier dropped a skier offered by Graeme Swann at long-on. Australia may have to try a couple of new, unscarred batsmen this winter.

There is a strange feature about Broad's delivery when he embarks on one of his headlong pursuits of big game, when he has scented blood and kicks up his knees as he runs in. In defiance of the orthodox instruction to keep his leading arm high, to point the way, Broad's left arm drops away, and the faster he bowls, the earlier it falls. In these moments, when on a roll, he is guided by passion rather than limbs.

And bowling fast is not all cruelty. In the process of running through Australia on a long evening under a northern sky, Broad helped out his mate, his hunting partner.

In the last two Tests James Anderson has gone through a more fallow period than at any time since England's 2006-07 tour of Australia, which resulted in the destruction of many reputations. Here he was driven like a medium pacer, and Australia would have knocked off the runs last evening, without losing a wicket, at the rate Anderson was going.

At Old Trafford and Riverside Anderson has taken four wickets for 291 – and the cloudy second day of this game was the prime time to bowl seam, as Broad demonstrated with his first innings figures of five for 71.

But last evening Broad covered for his partner. And for a source of inspiration he had that tour de force at Trent Bridge when Anderson had personally stood in the way of Australia's pursuit of 311.

It was fitting that, for an ending, Australia's last man hit a catch off Broad to mid-off, where Anderson caught and started England's celebrations.

August 13 Jim White

There was a moment on Monday when it became clear what an extraordinary day of cricket this was. As James Anderson came in to bowl to Usman Khawaja the sky behind him was coal black. Over his shoulder as he ran up, lightning sparked and sizzled in the distance.

All afternoon, glowering clouds had skidded past by on their way to drench Newcastle. And yet, on a day when amber flood warnings were hoisted over much of the North East, by some meteorological quirk, beyond a brief flurry over lunch, not a drop of rain fell on Chester-le-Street. Even the elements, it seemed, did not want a second of this unmissable drama to be disturbed.

This was Test cricket at its most compelling. All day the

momentum rocked giddily back and forth in the manner of the over-refreshed chap dressed as the Honey Monster tottering down the steps of the temporary stand to the bar. Just as one side thought they were in the ascendant, so the rhythm altered, the plot changed and a spring was injected into the step of their rivals.

It was exactly the kind of switchback day that gives the traditionalist the ammunition to argue the superiority of the long form game. How could anyone take thrash and dash seriously when this is what the real thing delivers?

And yet everywhere was evidence of the influence of one-day cricket on the five-day incarnation. In fact, it is legitimate to suggest that it was the attitudes bred and developed in the limited-over game that made this such a great day of Test match play.

After a harem scarem morning dash, in which Ryan Harris bowled like Dennis Lillee and Tim Bresnan did a compelling impression of a batsman, England set Australia a target of 299 to win.

In the past, that might have been regarded as an intimidating total, enough to make the side batting last retreat into a shell of attrition. But for those younger Aussies schooled in the Indian Premier League, it was the kind of figure they would be confident of chasing down in a Twenty20.

Take David Warner. A man largely previously defined by his one-day performances (not to mention extra-curricular stupidities) he began the afternoon apparently under the impression he was involved in a run gallop in Bangalore.

He hit Anderson, Bresnan and Stuart Broad with aplomb.

Soon, the Australian supporters in the stands had cast aside their distaste for his antics and were waving their prim-rose-coloured caps in signal of his fours.

Schooled as he may be in IPL rhythms, Warner played beautifully. He was not remotely intemperate or irresponsi-ble, invariably choosing the right ball to dispatch (his six off Graeme Swann was a collector's item).

And when he and Chris Rogers secured the first Australian century opening partnership in an Ashes test since Matthew Hayden and Justin Langer put on a ton at the Oval in 2005, it seemed all too plausible that he would lead his side to victory.

But then, entirely against the run of play, Bresnan pro-duced a ball not even Don Bradman at the peak of his powers could have survived. Warner was gone for 71. The moment his ball was caught by Matt Prior, England refound their mojo.

In the stands the volume was suddenly turned up. More to the point, Stuart Broad decided this was now the time to unleash his best. From 168 for two, Australia stumbled to 224 all out, splattered and scattered by Broad at his most devilish. As one-day chases went it all turned suddenly execrable; once their unlikely anchor had been withdrawn, Australia were sunk.

When, with the shadows lengthening around him, Broad persuaded Peter Siddle to scoop a catch to Anderson, it was over. England had won the series, their third on the bounce against the old enemy.

'Really interesting,' was the match winner's description of

the day. Interesting? Is that all? Broad is clearly as much a master of understatement as he is of seam.

This was magnificent. Warner's effort – which at one stage looked certain to land optimistic punters with a betting windfall – was suddenly undermined by what followed. And that is the beauty of Test cricket: you just never know what will happen.

August 13 Simon Hughes

The magic ball, the one that angles in to the batsman, pitches on a fullish length and moves suddenly away to beat him all ends up and remove his off stump, is the one all bowlers seek. It is like the curling 30-yard free kick into the top corner or the soaring drive 280 yards straight down the middle with a hint of draw. It happens once in a blue moon, if you are lucky.

The England bowlers have produced not one but two magic balls this summer. One by Jimmy Anderson at Trent Bridge. The other on Monday from Stuart Broad. It is Australia's misfortune that the recipient in each case was their captain Michael Clarke. Anderson did him for a duck in his first innings of the series at Trent Bridge. Broad castled him the ball after the drinks break yesterday afternoon.

It was a superbly executed wicket at the start of a rampaging spell. Finding a thundering rhythm from the Lumley Castle end and a hint of reverse swing, Broad had just produced a sharp bouncer that had brushed Clarke's glove before the break.

Now when play resumed at just after 6pm with Australia requiring 125 for victory and Clarke looking comfortable, Broad made quite a ploy of setting two men back on the hook, and a close fielder catching over Clarke's shoulder at leg gully. Was the bowler going to be predictable and bounce one at him, or be smarter and pitch it up?

He was smart. He unleashed the ball of the match. Delivered at sharp pace it homed in on middle-and-off stumps on a perfect length for a batsman back, expecting a short ball, rather than forward. It then bent away just enough in flight to slip past Clarke's groping bat and clip the off stump.

It was the kind of delivery that a batsman would struggle to play even if he knew it was coming. It not only damaged Clarke's wicket but broke Australia's back.

There is an element of luck in producing such deliveries. Every one of 1,000 tiny muscles and tendons have to be in perfect sync, the seam of the ball needs to be at exactly the right angle and flicked out so it is rotating backwards, the bowler's front leg has to straighten at precisely the right moment for maximum torque, his landing foot must be balanced and secure in the hole he has dug at the crease and the ball has to land on the optimum spot on the pitch to get the batsman hesitant about the length, playing from the crease expecting the ball to slant in. Then it has to swing at exactly the right moment in flight to beat the edge of the selected stroke. You can imagine why it does not happen often.

Such a ball gives the bowler a huge draught of confidence and a great vat of pride. He is buoyant and buzzing with energy. His feet float over the ground as he runs in for his next few balls. Fast bowling, a tough and painful job, feels at this moment like flying. It is sporting Nirvana.

Broad's pace increased – he was fizzing them down at 88-90mph and his optimism was total. The ball was reverse-swinging to his will. Steve Smith attempted a wild hook and dragged the ball into his stumps. Brad Haddin played across a straightish ball and was lbw. Ryan Harris went nowhere and was pinned in front. A big inswinger uprooted Nathan Lyon's leg stump. After a brief interlude for dim light during which the spinners were obliged to bowl, Broad persuaded Peter Siddle to lob a catch to mid-off. His demolition was complete.

It was irresistible bowling, superbly sustained, to go with his excellent perseverance in the first innings. And this from a guy who before the match was worried about a drain cover impeding his run up at the very end where yesterday he took six for 20 from 7.3 devastating overs. Which just goes to show that magic balls and spells happen when and where you least expect them. That is the beauty of sport.

August 14 Shane Warne

Three Tests in this series could have gone either way but the bottom line is England are 3-0 up and deserve to be because they are the better team. That is the beautiful thing about Test cricket, the strongest team will always win over the course of a series.

England have won the big moments but it was only when the realisation dawned that Australia were going to win the fourth Test in Durham that Alastair Cook started to be positive and aggressive.

The reason Australia had a chance was because of some bad bowling, some excellent batting and some very negative and defensive tactics from Cook. It stems back to the second innings in Manchester. It is as if England's first aim is not to lose rather than try to win.

Cook was way too cautious at the start of Australia's run chase. He had a deep point, would move slips out as soon as there was a good shot through the covers and the bowlers were bowling too short and not full and at the stumps. They were trying to defend with the ball and build pressure waiting for something to happen.

Off the field the frustration at his tactics was building. At one stage I saw David Saker, the bowling coach, go out and give some instructions. Andy Flower, the team director, walked down to give a message to the 12th man, which is very unusual as he likes to operate in the background.

Saker and Flower knew the team were losing the Test largely because of the captain's approach but the tea interval came at the right time for England. The break allowed them to get behind closed doors and regroup. They came out with a different mindset. They had the intent to take wickets and try to bowl Australia out.

Suddenly they started pitching the ball up, got some reverse swing somehow and it was a different game. Tim Bresnan took the big wicket of David Warner and then Stuart Broad bowled Michael Clarke and you sensed the whole momentum shift.

Once Clarke was out Australia went from favourites to England winning inside four days. Then it was no longer about the captain's tactics. It was about the bowlers making it happen. England won the Test because of some fine bowling and some poor shot selection, not because of brilliant captaincy.

Before the Test I criticised England for arrogance. I noticed a huge change in their attitude in Durham. Even a few people were saying hello out on the pitch and the interviews they gave during the game were completely different. Perhaps they got together and decided they had to change or it was the relief of retaining the Ashes in Manchester. Probably it was a combination of things but whatever the reason, they were a different bunch.

For Australia the result was very disheartening. When you look back they would have won in Manchester if it was not for the rain and in Durham they got themselves into a winning position but could not finish it off.

Some of the players did not have the bottle under pressure to handle the furnace out in the middle, the pressure of international cricket when the game is on the line. There are a few justifiable question marks over a few members of the Australian side. I reckon some of the players have one more chance to get it right in the fifth Test at the Oval.

Australia have to remember how to win. Getting into winning positions is only part of the job. It is that final step of crossing the line that matters. When you are on a bad run you lose that knack of winning. It is always hard to close a Test match out regardless of the situation. It takes nerve and bottle. It is a test of character. It is about having a calm, clear mind and knowing what to do in that situation.

When things are not going well you need to find a way to stop the momentum and get back into the game. That takes experience and unfortunately there are guys in the side who are inexperienced. They have not played a lot of first-class cricket, let alone international cricket.

The intensity at international level is completely different to first-class cricket. Also England have a quality bowling attack so there are no freebies when they get on a roll. At the Oval their personal pride and careers are on the line. It is also an opportunity to look at players before the next series starts at the Gabba in November. There is a lot at stake.

I feel for my mate Michael Clarke. When things are going badly you can sense the expectation that if he gets out the opposition think they will knock Australia over. It is quite hard for him to deliver all the time, especially when the pitches are nipping about a bit.

I know Durham will have hurt him. Rightly so, Australia were in a position to win. Hopefully the Australian players will remember how it felt and never want to be in that situation again.

Hopefully that inspires them to come out at the Oval next week and rediscover the winning feeling to set up the return bout in Australia.

Fifth Test The Oval Day One

August 22 Derek Pringle

Australia (307-4) v England

Not content with trying to win the Ashes series 4-0, England decided to give themselves a handicap for the final Test, handing debuts to two players hardly pressing for inclusion unless you had decided Australia could be beaten by fewer than 11 men.

Chris Woakes and Simon Kerrigan are having good county seasons for Warwickshire and Lancashire respectively, but their presence here, even on a dry pitch, was wholly unexpected given the presence of Chris Tremlett and Steven Finn in the same squad. Unsurprisingly, it was a situation Shane Watson took full advantage of to make 176, the highest Test score of his career, as Australia closed the first day delighted with their 307 for four.

Watson humiliated Kerrigan at Northampton last weekend when he struck him for seven fours and a six off 21 balls during the tour match against England Lions. He resumed the slaughter yesterday, smashing six fours off the spinner's first two overs. Nobody can be quite sure how a player will respond to nerves brought on by the big occasion but you would think that the clues in the Lions game might have struck a chord.

Kerrigan, 24, has come through the England and Wales Cricket Board's Performance Programme, so perhaps there was some pressure to promote from within. Those who have worked with him there since he was a teenager speak of his strong mentality and solid character, something that appeared to desert him yesterday.

He was not helped by captain Alastair Cook, who gave him a field for his first ball in Test cricket that screamed, 'I'm nervous for you.' A deep point for the long hop, a long off to stop the biff over the top along with a deep backward square for the more accepted sweep shot, should have been plenty of accident cover, yet Watson still found a way to notch up the boundaries. Whether he smelt Kerrigan's apprehension and decided to exploit it is unknown but it was brutal as he dismissed him to the midwicket rope.

Cook took him off after two overs but that was possibly a mistake as he would have begun his third against Chris Rogers, a blocker against whom he might have been able to settle. Instead he was allowed to fret for several hours before being summoned for a second spell just before tea, when any semblance of control seemed to desert him as he mixed long hops with a chest-high full toss.

All players experience nerves at some stage but like a tennis player's serve or a golfer's swing, bowlers need an action that is going to hold up under duress. Left-arm spinners seem particularly prone to the yips (something to do with the way their brains are wired up, apparently). With his short shuffle and lack of a strong front arm, Kerrigan has little time to find rhythm so it should not be a surprise when he fails to find any, as happened yesterday. Hopefully, after a better third spell saw him finish with eight overs for 53 runs, he will settle further to show his true capabilities.

There is nothing wrong with experimentation or blooding promising players, but this was just not the kind of team Andy Flower usually picks to win a Test match. The team director rarely has time for five-bowler attacks and the last time England picked two spinners at home was against Australia in Cardiff in 2009.

One theory was that Shane Warne's sledging, that England were dull and formulaic, had got to them and they were determined to beat Australia by different means. If true, they really need to rise above the baiting just as Darren Lehmann should have risen above the provocations of the Australian radio station which got him to bad-mouth Stuart Broad with the forlorn hope that Australian crowds this winter will send him home crying.

The juvenile banter did not upset Broad here and both he and James Anderson bowled well with the new ball, but only had David Warner's wicket to show for it. Rogers has grown in confidence since making telling contributions in the last two Tests but while he wore down the shine it was Watson who added the polish, racing to his fifty off just 61 balls. A spirited half-century is normally where it ends for Watson but his move to three – promotion is not the right word for his peripatetic shuffles up and down Australia's batting order – brought a determination to disprove those who have suggested he might be expendable. So while Michael Clarke, his captain, was given a brutal working over by Broad, from which Anderson benefited by bowling him through the gate, Watson continued unperturbed to his hundred save for a painful blow to the jaw when he ducked into a Broad bouncer.

It was his third Test hundred and his first since 2010. His conversion rate of fifties to hundreds is 12.5 per cent, one of the lowest of all leading batsmen apart from Pakistan's Rameez Raja, whose rate was eight per cent. But not every cricket fan in Australia felt pleased for him. One tweeted that it was typical of Watson to deliver once the series had gone.

Watson's powerful driving and his ability to pull off the front foot make him difficult to bowl at and he was the dominant partner in the two century stands he shared with Rogers (who contributed 20) and Steve Smith (38). Smith, who reached his fifty just before the second new ball was taken, batted well enough to follow Watson's lead in striking Graeme Swann for six back over the bowler's head.

Although dropped by Cook at slip off Anderson when on 104, Watson progressed to the point where a double hundred looked routine. But England took the second new ball and when Broad tested his mettle with another bouncer, Kevin Pietersen was on hand to snaffle the hook shot with a fine running catch at long leg.

Having picked up Warner with the new ball, Anderson's dismissal of Clarke saw him overtake Bob Willis in the pantheon of wicket-takers for England. He is now in second place behind Ian Botham, his 326 Test wickets still 51 short of overhauling the leader.

August 22 Simon Hughes

Before this Test England talked about being ruthless, seeking to go where no England team had been before and defeating Australia 4-0. Their team selection was seriously at odds with that intent.

They gave debuts to a seamer who had already looked overexposed for England in one-day cricket, and an inexperienced left-arm spinner who was milked for four an over by the Australians while playing for the England Lions last weekend.

On an admittedly flat Oval pitch, the combined figures of Chris Woakes and Simon Kerrigan of nought for 105 underline their ineffectiveness. Woakes was on in the 13th over after an outstanding spell from Jimmy Anderson that deserved more than the wicket of David Warner. Woakes's first over in Test cricket was tidy, if unthreatening.

The last ball, slightly short, was eagerly deposited into the midwicket fence by Shane Watson. His second over was polite, the equivalent of a trainee turning up for his first day at the office minding his p's and q's.

Once he had got the measure of Woakes, Watson dispatched him for three boundaries off his third. By the time he was removed after five innocuous overs, the score had more than doubled to 64 for one and Watson was into his stride.

That was Kerrigan's misfortune. Watson had already taken to the left-arm spinner with relish in the Lions match, and now Alastair Cook summoned him to bowl.

Like a Rottweiler sensing a nervous postman, the Australian recognised his opponent's apprehension immediately, and it was shared by Cook, who gave him a deep cover and a long off from the start.

It did not prevent Watson thumping a boundary off his third ball, a low full toss, and whipping another through midwicket off his fifth.

Usually a debutant breathes a sigh of relief after getting his first over out of the way. Kerrigan's nerves increased. His eighth ball was slow and pitched woefully short. Watson had time to lay back, count the leg-side fielders, and smack it between them. With calculated intent he advanced up the pitch to the next and drove it over the top for four.

His whole body now taut with tension, Kerrigan stuttered to the wicket almost reluctant to reach the crease. The last two deliveries were not bowled. They fell out of his hand and were both savaged to the midwicket boundary. Two overs for 28 left Cook with no option but to withdraw him. Australia were 103 for one – Watson 76 not out – and completely in charge. It was an initiative they never sacrificed.

Woakes's later spells were at least steady. His line and length was consistent. His problem is he does very little with the ball. He jogs in willingly, lets the ball go at a reasonable pace. But he resembles a bowling machine, presenting the ball on an amiable length, inviting driving practice. It was frequently accepted by Watson.

Kerrigan was given another chance by the sympathetic Cook. One over featured a head-high full toss, another a couple of long hops that were so bad the batsmen could not hit them. They almost bounced twice. It was horrible to watch.

What exacerbated his problem was his jerky, abbreviated action. A spinner needs to use his body and a full follow through to impart spin and disguise his variations of pace. Bad balls can be partly camouflaged.

Yesterday Kerrigan barely used his front arm and flicked rather than bowled the ball with a very short trajectory. There was no hint of deception. He suffered a minor form of the yips.

The chairman of selectors, Geoff Miller, well remembers a Derbyshire left-armer, Fred Swarbrook, who suffered the same affliction.

He saw a faith healer, who advised him to keep a lucky pebble in his pocket. When he continued to bowl double bouncers and full tosses his captain said: 'Fred, get rid of the ball and try bowling the pebble!' It is to be hoped that one of England's array of backroom staff can find a cure for Kerrigan and quick.

August 22 Paul Hayward

Darren Lehmann's call to the Australian public to hound Stuart Broad this winter just goes to show that a statesman's robes are bound to look not quite right on a man who answers to the nickname of 'Shrek'.

Exhorting the mob to make Broad's life hell in the return series was either Lehmann's way of disguising the poverty of the resources at his disposal or a lapse into the yard-dog tendencies of his playing career. In any case it was unpleasant.

Imagine if modern crowds constantly reminded Australia's

coach of his own big transgression, in 2003, when he was banned for five one-day games for a 'racially motivated obscenity' after he had been run out by Sri Lanka.

"Black c----" is the epithet Lehmann was punished for barking 10 years ago.

Despite the scandal at the time, the incident did not impede his progress in cricket.

His appointment as Australia coach two weeks before this Ashes series began was widely popular in his home country. No reference was made to his racial outburst a decade back.

So why raise it now? To make the point that those who are well acquainted with crime and punishment ought not to invoke the wrath of the masses against a fellow professional whose only sin was to extend the modern norm of not walking when ball clips bat. That, and taking his boot off to kill time, and being a general irritant to Australians.

In the context of cricket's modern ills, Broad is hardly Nosferatu, even if there was a legitimate case for arguing that he ought to have walked at Trent Bridge after directing a thick edge off Ashton Agar to first slip via the wicketkeeper's gloves.

Never mind that Lehmann can claim some measure of provocation. Earlier this week, with a 3-0 series win secure, Broad said: 'Yes, I knew I'd hit it. But if you go through the series and look at the Australian players who have nicked it and not walked you could name several – Warner, Rogers, Khawaja, Smith, Clarke, Agar. I mean it's quite a lot of players for it to be a big issue. Why are people picking on me? Well, it's the way our media works I suppose.'

During an interview with the Australian rock network, Triple M, Lehmann clearly decided that Broad's attempt at moral equivalence could not be tolerated. 'He's been copping it all series, mate,' the coach told the presenter. 'I expect it will continue for a long time yet and I would hope the public get stuck into him when he gets out to Australia. I hope he whinges a lot.'

The presenter then went on to suggest Broad could expect a fruity reception around Australia's boundary ropes. 'Certainly our players haven't forgotten, they're calling him everything under the sun as they go past,' Lehmann said. 'I hope the Australian public are the same because that was just blatant cheating. I don't advocate walking but when you hit it to first slip it's pretty hard. From my point of view I just hope the Australian public give it to him right from the word go for the whole summer and I hope he cries and he goes home. I just hope everyone gets stuck into him because the way he's carried on and the way he's commented in public about it is ridiculous.'

'He knew he hit it to slip. The biggest problem there is the poor umpire cops all the crap that he gets in the paper and Stuart Broad makes him look like a fool. From my point of view it's poor, so I hope the public actually get stuck into him.'

An odd mix of macho man and fun-loving tension-de-fuser, Lehmann inherited a thankless task with this Australia squad and has endured many frustrations on the road to the Oval.

Charitably, England took the heat off their old enemy here

with an experimental bowling line-up that helped Australia pile up 307 for four and featured a rare century (176) from Shane Watson, usually a master of self-sabotage.

There is an escalating risk that England have thrown away their chance of an unprecedented 4-0 Ashes win by picking Chris Woakes and Simon Kerrigan for this Test.

The result has been to dump all the wicket-taking responsibilities on Broad, James Anderson and Graeme Swann, with the possibility that Australia could win this Oval Test and claim the momentum for this winter's series.

Lehmann's tirade against Broad – which, by seeking to make a pariah of a visiting sportsman, far exceeds the normal Ashes sledging – could be seen as the first exchange in the battle of Brisbane, where the next series starts on Nov 21.

But there is little sign of psychological frailty in Broad, to whom all narrative paths seem to have led this summer.

With Lehmann's words in his ears, Broad almost knocked Watson's block off with a bouncer when he was on 91, and then finally took his wicket when Kevin Pietersen took a diving catch in the deep.

The limelight seems to like Broad.

The same could not be said of Lehmann, who was ticked off by Jim Maxwell, that fine Australian commentator. 'It sounds a bit like pub talk,' Maxwell said. 'But he is the Australia team coach and he should be a little more careful.' A sanction would be in order.

This is a transcript of an interview with Australia's coach Darren Lehmann on Australian radio station Triple M:

Loose talk: How 'Boof' got stuck in to the England pace man on Aussie radio.

DJ   Now Boof, Stuart Broad has come out and started speaking about the fact that he nicked that ball all those Test matches ago, so we go: 'Thanks Stuart, thanks for the tip on that one.' But I loved what he said after that, and you might not have picked up on it. He said, 'Look, I'm sure by the time the team arrives in November in Australia that all the Australian public will have forgotten about that,' and he won't get a hard time. Well, if you see Stuart could you just let him know that we've got pretty big memories here and we haven't forgotten?

DARREN LEHMANN   Certainly our players haven't forgotten, they're calling him everything under the sun as they go past, so I would hope that the Australian public are the same, because that was just blatant cheating. You know, I don't advocate walking, but when you hit it to first slip it's pretty hard. So from my point of view, I hope that the Australian public just give it to him right from the word go for the whole summer, and I hope he cries and goes home.

DJ   The first day at the Gabba is Free Tomato Day, they're giving tomatoes out outside the ground, so just let him know that would you, Boof?

DL   Perfect, we'll get the whole lot for him. I just hope everyone gets stuck into him because the way he's carried on and the way he's commented in public about it, I mean it's ridiculous – he knew he hit it to slip. The biggest problem there is that the poor umpire cops all the crap that he gets in the paper, and Stuart Broad makes him look like a fool.

From my point of view that's poor, so I hope the public actually get stuck into him.

Day Two

August 23 Derek Pringle

Australia (492-9d) lead England (32-0) by 460 runs

If this was England's plan to scar Australia in readiness for the return Ashes series in three months time it has backfired spectacularly. Instead of inflicting inner turmoil they have put a spring back into the Aussie's step, one personified by the jaunty swagger of Steve Smith after he brought up his maiden Test hundred with a six.

Smith's unbeaten 138, a large slice of his team's 492-9 declared, has suddenly placed England under pressure after they finished the day on 32 for none, still trailing their opponents by 460 runs.

They may well have won the Investec Ashes convincingly, but victory will seem hollow if the urn is hoisted having had the worst of this Test, as now seems likely following the surprising selection of Chris Woakes and Simon Kerrigan.

With rain delaying yesterday's start until 2.30pm and with low cloud seemingly anchored to the gasometer, Kerrigan was not given the chance to reprieve himself in the 38.5 overs England managed before Australia's declaration.

Instead it was the seamers, Woakes included, who did the bulk of the work, if that is what you can call it when the overrate is a dilatory 11 overs an hour – which it was after tea.

If England have been chastened by how their two debutants have fared so far, their mood would not have improved when they learned that Chris Tremlett had taken 5-51 against Durham for Surrey.

Apparently, Tremlett was set to play here until the groundsman at the Kia Oval, Lee Fortis, shaved the pitch early on the first morning of the match. With the sun blazing, the surface suddenly looked very different and Kerrigan was pressed hastily into action, a rapid promotion he did not appear ready for. Groundsman can do what they like to the pitch, within reason, before they hand it over half an hour before the start.

Surrey have sold out all five days of the match but there would have been no pressure from them to produce what is known in the business as a 'chief executive's pitch', as they have insured their gate in case of an early finish.

Whatever properties this strip has, it was to the liking of Smith who was scarcely inconvenienced as he went to his hundred, and beyond, with a swagger. At 24, he is the youngest Australian to score a maiden Ashes century since a 22-year old Ricky Ponting made one at Headingley in 1997.

Smith does not have the same poise and class at the crease as Ponting but he is a feisty competitor who, but for a bout of impatience at Old Trafford, could have had two hundreds this series, an achievement that would have knelt only to Ian Bell's three centuries.

He reached the milestone in swashbuckling style, with a straight six off Jonathan Trott. After his loss of patience at Old Trafford, following a period of stasis where he became bogged down, he decided to let his instincts rule here.

Trott pitched up, Smith's eyes lit up, the bat was swung with intent, and off it went, deep among the spectators at the Vauxhall End.

His success, here and in the rest of the series, is a small triumph for Darren Lehmann, who pushed for his inclusion after he was left out of the original squad. Australia's coach, thrust into the job when Mickey Arthur was sacked 17 days before the series began, has not had much go right, some of it self-inflicted, but Smith is one project he can take some pride from.

He might also point out, when he is not inciting the mob against Stuart Broad, that Australia have twice passed 400 in the series, a threshold England have yet to cross despite winning three of the four Tests played. Instead, Cook's teams have won the big moments that settle matches, and that has proved defining.

On Thursday, the big moment for England would have been in preventing Australia reaching 400, but that plan soon morphed into one where the overrate was slowed after Smith showed he was not for the taking.

He needed to bat well especially when Anderson produced a beauty that pitched middle and hit off to bowl Peter Siddle. It was the kind of ball Geoffrey Boycott would say was wasted on a tail-ender but Anderson has struggled for dominance since Lord's and he would have taken it with gratitude.

Although he, Broad and Woakes tried to harness the cloud cover in pursuit of swing, it was Trott, three balls after being hit for six by Smith, who struck next after Brad Haddin chopped a cut shot onto his stumps.

That Cook even turned to Trott when he had five bowlers at his disposal was testament to England's selection boo-boo. But while Woakes had a better day with the ball, even snaffling his first Test wicket after James Faulkner hit out prior to the declaration, he still looked a trick short for Test cricket.

When Cook did eventually introduce spin in the form of Graeme Swann, the off-spinner bowled a swiping Mitchell Starc with his second ball. But when Ryan Harris twice deposited him over the rope for six he was quickly withdrawn and it was left to Anderson to dismiss him and gain his fourth wicket of the innings, the one small positive for England in a Test that was negatively charged from the moment they announced their team.

August 23 Paul Hayward

After the parade of celebs at Lord's, Test Match Special had to make do with a former governor of the Bank of England. Mervyn King's presence in the commentary box expressed the shortage of glamour in a match where England had promised to pummel Australia into the ground but offered tea and counselling instead.

The Oval has become synonymous with Anglo-Australian endgames. In 2005 and again four years later the great cricket contest expired on this ground like summer itself. Back then the urn was in the balance. A nation felt the full rush of intoxication and wondered how they would cope without the Ashes.

Now, there is no sign of Damien Lewis, David Cameron, Jude Law or Ed Miliband at the TMS mic. The country watches listlessly, even booing England's slow over rate. But at the heart of this final ritual is the old question of momentum. When several England players sparked up fags after beers to celebrate their 3-0 series victory in Durham it was the start of a new phase. Andy Flower's team might be cruel or they could be kind in south London. In the event they put the kettle on for Australia.

When the story of this series is filed the decision to promote Chris Woakes and Simon Kerrigan for a Test that offered England a chance to secure a unique 4-0 win will take high rank on the list of subjects requiring further explanation.

'No mercy' was the theme of the build-up. No let-up. Revenge would be taken for all those years of Aussie sadism, when the battering would not cease until the plane was heaving clear of Sydney. England made all the right noises about making history but then chose to open the gate to Australia instead.

After 9 hr 32 min the Baggy Green innings finally ended at 492 for nine declared. Across that rain-spattered epoch all kinds of comforts were extended to Michael Clarke's men. First, Shane Watson was helped across the canyon of a rare Test century. He fed on the freeze-afflicted Kerrigan. Watson was even able to brush up his terrible review decision making along the way. On day two, with autumn nibbling at the edges, England accompanied Steve Smith to his first Test century.

Both batsmen will take happy memories of the Oval to Brisbane in November and believe they can hurt England's bowlers again. These are big advances. Watson, who bludgeoned 176, has now overcome his addiction to false starts. Smith, who looked unprepared for this level earlier in the series, will feel like a middle-order fixture. He may even fancy himself as the coming man of Australian batting. James Faulkner, 23, made his mark with an entertaining knock the same size as his age, swiping three fours off Stuart Broad after tea as England conceded 47 runs in five overs.

Across Australia's squad, few will leave feeling like failures. Mitchell Starc is a bowler of promise and an imposing tail-end batsman. Ryan Harris has puffed his chest and displayed his quality. Chris Rogers has assumed the role of vindicated veteran. David Warner has come in from the cold to parade his skills without yet fully settling down.

With their 3-0 lead, England will have been hoping to wipe out any Australian gains in this match, but a weakened bowling attack blew that opportunity. Woakes, whose vertigo subsided, was competent without being threatening. His one wicket, a catch on the boundary, from 24 overs, cost 96 runs. Poor Kerrigan was sent up the line to a grisly fate: eight overs on Wednesday at a cost 53, and not a single ball yesterday, when Jonathan Trott was asked to trundle in ahead of him. Kerrigan's selection both undermined England's prospects and threatened to destroy his confidence. Not bowling him at all yesterday was a failure of logic and compassion. All it did was emphasise the error of picking him in the first place.

With Broad and James Anderson carrying the seam-bowling load, and Swann held back, England attempted to stem the bleeding by slowing the over rate, with Swann constantly drying the ball for Broad like Andy Murray mopping his brow on Centre Court. The umpires were oblivious, or indifferent. England bowled 11.5 overs in 64 minutes. Boos rose from the Australian contingent but also from England fans, who wanted entertainment.

With Cook's team so ragged, their openers were vulnerable to assault by Clarke's bowlers. There was a lightness about Australia that spoke of rising hopes for the winter. For most of the summer they have walked round the rim of humiliation's volcano. But they look a far more coherent side than at Lord's, when they were lampooned as the worst to come up our beaches.

In team selection, and motivation, England have fallen short of the pre-Test rhetoric about leaving marks in history. This is an impenetrable, sometimes remote England side, who are either blind to the dangers of surrendering the initiative so close to a winter series or perhaps so confident of their superiority that they have written this match off as an irrelevance, if only subconsciously.

Either way it is not what was promised, or expected by the crowd, who have learned that the Oval is not always an Ashes crucible. Summer's bird has flown.

August 23 Scyld Berry

Another piece of Australia's jigsaw fell into place on Thursday. Steve Smith, by making his maiden Test century, sealed the fifth batting slot in their top six for the return Ashes this winter.

Smith is the fourth Australian to make a hundred in this series: the tourists have scored four in all, against England's five, yet they are lagging 3-0 behind.

A correlation between team success and individual centuries is commonly perceived, but it did not apply either in the last Ashes series in England in 2009, when Australia beat England 8-2 in centuries and lost 2-1 in match results.

Beyond and better than numbers, Smith lit up the second day of the final Test as England slowed the game down, until a wan sun joined him after tea in supplementing the Oval's floodlights.

It has not been a bright or smiley series: England, burdened with the label of outright favourites, have gone about proving as much with stern determination on slow pitches. But Smith is too jaunty and boyish to be a party to attritional grimness.

At the close of play, as the Australians left the field, Smith was ushered forward by his team-mates in the age-old tradition to lead them off. He smiled – almost beamed – the smile of a fresh-faced and uncynical 24-year-old, before bouncing up the steps like Tigger.

It has taken almost a whole generation for Australia to find an answer to Derek Randall, the Nottinghamshire batsman who played the innings of his life in the Centenary Test

of 1977, but at last they have. For not only does Smith dis-
turb the gravity of a Test match with his smiling, like Randall
did: he fidgets every bit as much too.

A more fidgety fidget than Smith, indeed, has probably
never played a Test match. He veers to the opposite extreme
of England's captain Alastair Cook, who is impassive and
minimalist in his movements.

When Smith takes a run – and he is electric between the
wickets – his limbs fly in several directions simultaneously.
But he does not stop to draw breath if it is his turn to take
strike: oh no, having done his running, he embarks upon a
routine that is tiring to watch once, never mind to repeat
several hundred times.

First Smith marks his guard again, several times over, by
sawing his bat through the crease's earth. Imagine Jonathan
Trott going through his repertoire – his tour de force – before
his first ball, then fast-forward it, and Smith does that every
ball.

After re-marking his guard, and giving his partner a
thumbs-up if his partner has scored the last run, Smith pats
his helmet more than once with his left glove, checks his box
is in place, touches each of his pads, and fiddles with both
gloves. Only then does he get down to patting his bat in the
crease, which has to be worth at least half a dozen nervous
twitches.

So between a dozen and 20 distinct manual movements
and gestures are required between each delivery that
Smith faces. And if the bowler should abort his run-up
or other delays arise – as England made sure they did by

asking the umpires every few minutes whether the ball was too damp – then Smith has to go through his routine again.

When he emerged for New South Wales as a leg-spinner who batted, Smith was one of several to be labelled Shane Warne's successor. (He could not bowl off-spin: far less energy would be involved.) But Australian cricket was losing great batsmen, and vacancies arose, so Tigger put up his paw.

His 77 against Pakistan in the Headingley Test of 2010 was the first hint of his batting potential. It was a witty innings, played on a difficult pitch with tail-enders for company: he had to find a way to score quickly, and he used his wits to do so.

In the interim Smith has tightened his defence. He now bends his front knee, instead of keeping it stiff, which has reduced the gap between his bat and pad. He has sobered a little, without losing that Randallesque exuberance.

And when he reached 94, the enfant terrible could be restrained no more. Fast hands, good footwork, some boyish panache flavoured by a fit of impishness, all combined to hit Trott straight back over his head for six. At the tea interval shortly afterwards, he no doubt bounced up the pavilion steps into the Australian dressing room and asked for honey.

Day Three
August 24 Derek Pringle

England (247-4) trail Australia (492-9d) by 245 runs

Not content with subverting modern over-rates to slow the game to a crawl when Australia batted on day two, England adopted old-fashioned scoring rates yesterday in a determined attempt to kill the final Investec Test match by creating a stalemate.

It made for a flat day's play in which England's top order added 215 runs in 98.3 overs. With two days remaining they trail Australia by 245 runs, needing another 46 to avoid the follow-on.

The last time scoring rates were this low was in the 1950s when the average scoring rate was 2.3 runs per over, a figure England undercut here by rumbling along at 2.13 runs for every six balls bowled as they plodded after Australia's first innings total of 492. The 1950s made up for the sloth with an over rate of 20 per hour, a frequency England almost halved here in what some are seeing as a snub to the paying public. 'It was the worst sporting entertainment I've ever seen,' said the former England rugby player Simon Halliday, who was one of those watching.

Even Kevin Pietersen entered into the drudgery, which was catching. His 50, made off 133 balls, was his slowest half-century in an Ashes series and his third slowest in all Tests, its pedantic nature at odds with the feisty exchange he had with Australia's captain, Michael Clarke.

Although Joe Root made a worthy 68, Pietersen's exchange of views with Clarke just before tea, and just after Australia took the second new ball, were the most exciting moments in a dreary day's cricket. With neither man an intellectual giant this was badinage of the most basic kind as each man pointed out the other's lack of popularity among team-mates.

For Pietersen there was none of the direct messaging that got him into so much trouble this time last year, just one direct message, from Clarke. During the lunch break, Pietersen was presented with a silver bat in recognition of him being England's batsman with the most international runs, his 13,320 runs made in Tests, one-day internationals and T20s exceeding the 13,290 made by Graham Gooch in the first two of those formats.

Some believe this will be Pietersen's last Ashes Test in England and while it has always been his aim to score 10,000 Test runs – a project that would incorporate the next home Ashes series in 2015 – he has looked more than his age this series as the aches and pains have mounted.

He might have made better headway towards that goal had he tried to dominate Australia's bowlers as he did here in 2005. Instead, he allowed little things like people moving in the crowd to distract him, the net effect being an innings that was wholly unrepresentative of him with its quartet of fours. It fizzled out too, the umpires reviewing what looked like a straightforward catch to Shane Watson at first slip, off Mitchell Starc, after Pietersen suggested it might have been a bump ball. TV replays showed it was not and the capacity crowd's best hope of some belated entertainment went with him as he trudged off.

England's sluggish intentions began with Root and Alastair Cook, who despite the caution chalked up their first half-century partnership of the series. The disciplined approach of Australia's bowlers throughout the series has made both men work hard for their runs and spectators work even harder for those moments of ecstasy that make a day at the Test worthwhile, and worth the money.

Australia's control paid off when Cook became impatient and allowed his bat to get ahead of his pad as he pushed at one from Ryan Harris outside his off stump. It was a failing Australia managed to exploit in the 2006/7 series and again in 2009 when he averaged in the mid-twenties. Of course, in the last Ashes Cook had an incredible series with the bat, blazing a record-breaking trail, but this one has seen him regress to the figures and mistakes of those earlier series.

Root needed a good innings just to leave Australia a parting memento of his talent before they all meet up again at the Gabba on Nov 21.

After his 180 in the second innings at Lord's he has looked timid, lacking in the youthful zest and confidence that epitomised his early innings. At 22, his form is bound to ebb and flow a bit but yesterday he looked in command again until he top-edged a sweep off Nathan Lyon to Watson at backward square leg.

Jonathan Trott also needed a score and he almost got one. Seeing off Australia's leg theory, which he has succumbed to on a couple of occasions, he was looking as fluent as is possible in the context of England's crawl when Starc got his swing geometry right with the second new ball and had him lbw.

The sluggish pitch has not helped produce dynamic cricket. Batsmen in fine form, such as Ian Bell, have been able to time it, but those searching for form have needed to wait long for the bad ball. There are signs that the pitch is beginning to turn with both Lyon and Steve Smith finding some spin and bounce. But they have been too sporadic for England not to save the follow-on today.

Once that has occurred, it will probably be down to Australia to risk a four-nil loss to entice England to play a shot in anger, something they have not managed to do yet.

August 24 Paul Hayward

Kevin Pietersen was slow with his bat and quick with his mouth when Australia tried to portray him as a pariah in this England side.

'No one likes you, Kevin,' is what Michael Clarke is believed to have told him when a sometimes soporific day flared into crowd-pleasing rancour. At last, some Ashes edge. There have been sporadic skirmishes in this series but the two teams have mostly steered clear of industrial-scale sledging. Chortling in the Test Match Special commentary box as Pietersen and Clarke set about each other was Phil Tufnell, who was once asked by an Australian tormentor: 'Hey, Tufnell, can I borrow your brain? I'm building an idiot.'

This time, the flashpoint is thought to have been a distinctly retro attempt to soften up Ian Bell, a favourite target of the baggy greens. Have they not been reading the scoreboard? Bell's imperious batting has been England's greatest asset in this series. To taunt him for being milky these days is like putting a Buddy Holly record on at a rave.

But Pietersen, who was removed as England captain in 2009, jumped into the leader's role to stick up for the stylish and newly toughened Bell. That caused Clarke to shout a challenge from first slip to the non-striker's end, and Pietersen to reply, according to reports: 'No one likes you either, and you're the captain.'

This battle between the two 'metrosexuals' to depict each other as outcasts was not only entertaining but informative. It said that Australia have been frustrated to hell and back in this Test. Desperate for a win to swing the pendulum back their way, they endured tardy English bowling on Thursday, then an attempt by Pommy batsmen to kill the game before the expected rain sets in today.

The Oval is Pietersen's stage. He was bound to control the narrative as he endeavoured to draw level with Herbert Sutcliffe as the only batsman to score five Test centuries on this ground. He shares his tally of four with Len Hutton, Wally Hammond and David Gower. Before joining the England innings he was presented with an encased silver bat as his country's leading scorer in all formats. His 13,320 runs since 2004 have included 23 Test centuries: two fewer than Alastair Cook.

A Surrey player now, Pietersen was sure to radiate a proprietorial air on the turf where he made his worldwide breakthrough with a majestic innings of 158 not out in 2005. His return to the England fold after the South Africa text-message farrago was pragmatic on both sides. If his relationship with the other players lacks a certain bonhomie, nobody could question his attitude or professionalism in this series, except in press conferences, where he has displayed glaring hostility to the media.

As if to emphasise his willingness to support the team (and thereby extend his Test career), Pietersen obeyed the party line, defying Australia's efforts to hurry them into following on. His fifty came off 127 balls and took 180 minutes. It was his slowest in the Ashes. Only once did he fully free his arms, ending a spell of 11 overs without a boundary to lift the ball back over Steve Smith's head.

Across the innings, England scored at 2.12 an over. A late ticket purchase for this third day would have cost you £199 on the internet. Watching this final Test has been a bit like reading the credits after a night at the cinema. Australia are desperate to win after their big first-innings total. England, who promised a scorched-earth end to the series, are content not to lose.

With this aim in mind, Pietersen adopted a belligerent stance at the crease but declined to use his weapon. The spat with Clarke was probably just what he wanted to satisfy his adrenalin need for the day. Australia decided before this series not to provoke L'Etranger on the grounds that it would be counter-productive. The theory is that Pietersen likes being yapped at because it helps him concentrate and appeals to his macho side.

But Clarke could not contain his own combative urges in the 81st over, when umpire Aleem Dar had to tell them all to cease and desist. Both umpires converged on the two England batsmen to discuss the contretemps. In the next over Ryan Harris made a point of glaring at Pietersen and both groups sidled off for tea fighting the temptation to start it up again.

A day after Australia's coach, Darren Lehmann, was fined for urging the Australian public to demonise Stuart Broad in the winter, Clarke seized his opportunity to roust his own troops by separating Pietersen from the herd.

Australia's captain knows that Pietersen cannot be rattled by a bit of chirping about his popularity rating in the England dressing room. The purpose was probably to encourage his own men to be more aggressive when the old enemies converge again in Brisbane on Nov 21 for the return series.

Soon, Australia were rid of the Oval cavalier. Pietersen dabbed at a Mitchell Starc delivery outside his off stump and clipped the ball to Shane Watson at slip. Before that, he had instructed spectators at both ends of the ground to sit down with all the grumpiness of a cold and hungry nightclub bouncer. For England, it is no bad thing to see him in this mood. If no one likes him, he hardly seems to care.

August 24 Scyld Berry

It had to be done. At Old Trafford England had batted too slowly under the mountain of scoreboard pressure. At the Oval they have batted in the way that has given them their best chance of drawing – not winning, of course, but drawing – the fifth Test.

Hard to beat, however, is also hard to watch. We cannot have it both ways. A run-rate of 2.12 an over is not what a Bank Holiday weekend crowd wanted, but their disapproval of ironic cheering was mild compared to the criticism which would have been fired at England if they had been dismissed for 280 in 80 overs and were now following on.

Suppose Joe Root had nicked an expansive drive at Ryan Harris for another low score, instead of setting himself up for the tour of Australia, or Jonathan Trott had been caught hooking his way out of trouble against the short ball, or Alastair Cook had been bowled reverse-sweeping. All merry stuff, but the dissatisfaction – of knowing that England could have tried harder and done better – would have been captured on history's page and forever rankled.

There was a host of reasons – not excuses – for England not getting out of second gear. Their top three are out of nick, the ball is not coming on for the drive, it is bouncing for the spinners, and their selection has weakened their batting as well as their bowling. Having a debutant all-rounder at six, and a wicketkeeper in the worst batting run of his Test career, made the five specialist batsmen even more cautious. Since New Zealand, Matt Prior has been averaging 14.

Above all though, Australia bowled as well as they could have, and pretty close to superlatively. They bowled in exactly the way that each England batsman least liked. Full with a bit of width to Cook; full on off stump to Root; more than the odd bouncer for Trott, who was struck again. If Michael

Clarke's back had allowed, he would have bowled his slow left-armers at Kevin Pietersen.

James Faulkner is not a Test bowler – T20s yes, and one-dayers perhaps – but that still left Ryan Harris, backed by the accuracy of Peter Siddle and the odd magic ball from Mitchell Starc, while Nathan Lyon got more out of the day-three pitch than Graeme Swann on the first two days.

So if we want a 'dead-rubber Test' to be treated with the same seriousness as a live Test, England's only option was batting that veered between low-risk and no-risk. The two T20 internationals are to be seen on Thursday at the Ageas Bowl and at Riverside on Saturday.

Ashes Tests have never been slapstick. Sure, Len Hutton scored 364 in "the good old days", but when England racked up 903 for seven at the Oval in 1938 their run-rate was 2.69 an over, only half a run higher than yesterday's rate.

Factor in Australia's superlative fielding too. If David Warner had been sprinting after the ball in 1938, diving headfirst, clawing it back, leaping up then firing it with a bullet's trajectory to the keeper, England's run-rate would have been very 'adjacent' – as John Arlott would have said – to 2.12.

Even when Don Bradman went to town, the scoring rate was barely higher in terms of runs per over. While thumping England for 232 at the Oval in 1930, he gave Douglas Jardine such food for thought that he conceived Bodyline, but Australia still averaged no more than 2.71 an over.

Better to turn it round and say that England have done well not to lose more than four wickets in 116 overs so far;

that Pietersen yesterday played his most selfless innings yet in the team's cause, perhaps one that he could not have achieved without last year's warning shot across his bows; and that England, to date, have not lost a Test this calendar year.

Day Four
August 25 Scyld Berry

No play due to rain

Should England lose fewer than 16 wickets on Sunday, they will equal their best result in an Ashes series at home.

Moreover, when England won 3-0 in 1977, Australian cricket was in a state of serious schism because half of their team had signed for the World Series and the other half had not, while in 1886 Australian cricket had no national governing body to organise and select their team.

This series is not quite over yet, however, because a minimum of 98 overs are scheduled for the final day, and the very prospect of going down as the equal-biggest losers in their history will spur Michael Clarke's Australia to produce one last effort.

Australia first have to prevent England scoring 46 more runs to reach their follow-on target of 293. After the pitch has been under cover for two nights and Saturday's wash-out, Australia's pace bowlers are likely to find it a suitable morning for swing and seam, so Ian Bell's job is not yet completed even though he is averaging 75.

The rest of England's batting consists of two debutants in Chris Woakes and Simon Kerrigan, a wicketkeeper who has scored 86 runs in this series, and the two older heads of Stuart Broad and Graeme Swann. As the self-styled engine-room of this England side, Matt Prior, Broad and Swann need to rev up this morning for England to finish on a high note.

After conceding 30 in his first five overs, Woakes has settled in as the game has gone on. Kerrigan's chance of redemption lies in England saving the follow-on handsomely, then Australia batting out the last few overs without anything left to play for, when he would have the chance of a rehabilitating bowl.

Even so, England's selection here has been proved wrong: the intention, without question, was to pick the 11 best equipped in the selectors' opinion to win this match, but the consequence was to throw an added weight on to the shoulders of James Anderson, just as the selection of Steve Finn ahead of Tim Bresnan did in the opening Test at Trent Bridge, Bresnan's most successful ground.

If England only just save the follow-on, Michael Clarke would still have one last dice to throw in his attempt to avoid doing down in Australian history alongside Greg Chappell and Hugh Scott, his two unillustrious predecessors.

Ten to 20 overs of hitting by David Warner and Shane Watson would then give Clarke enough runs to set a declaration, and the best part of two sessions to bowl England out a second time. Anderson and Broad would slow England's over rate down, but not so much as to risk a penalty for their captain Alastair Cook.

However low that declaration target is, England will not be keen to embark on a run-chase. But having been criticised widely for their defensiveness in this match – Australia's debutant James Faulkner suggested last night that spectators on Friday should be given their money back – there could come a point when England would feel embarrassed not to chase: if Clarke set 200 in 60 overs, for example, they might feel obliged to have a go.

Clarke will vividly remember how England wobbled when they had to bat out the last day of the third Test at Old Trafford. They had slumped to 37 for three against Ryan Harris and Peter Siddle before rain drew a veil.

But the luck in this series is forecast to favour England until the very last as showers are predicted. The pattern has been astonishingly consistent: when England have won the toss and batted first, they have won, but when Australia have won the toss and piled up a big total, rain has helped England to draw.

If England do avoid defeat on Sunday, they will go second in the ICC Test rankings above India and below South Africa. Australia will go fifth, behind Pakistan in fourth place, whatever Sunday's result.

Graham Gooch says England need to improve in all areas when the Ashes are played in Australia at the end of the year. 'We will be working very, very hard to make sure we improve when we go down to Australia – we need to improve,' said the England coach. 'The beauty of Test cricket [is] having a side that can win in any conditions – whatever pitches Australia produce we will be ready for that. We know that to beat Australia in their own back yard we are going to have to be a lot better both with the bat and the ball.'

August 25 Scyld Berry

It has been one of the less entertaining Ashes. England have won, and won well, but not in a way that will attract millions from 20-over cricket and the Indian Premier League.

The greatest drama happened on the last day at Trent Bridge, when James Anderson roused himself beyond concert-pitch to prevent Australia's last-wicket pair staggering over the line. And when the climax of a series comes in the opening Test, the rest is bound to be downhill.

England had no say in the shape of this narrative – indeed it was Australia's fault for collapsing at Lord's so that the bottom fell out of this series. England were always outright favourites, and when Graeme Swann reduced Australia from 42 without loss to 128 all out in their first innings, the outcome was all but sealed, with no fluctuations.

But where England had a say in this drama was in the set-up of the stages, and here the pitches were far too samey. England held the trump-card in Swann, and they played it in every single Test on very dry turners that were slow or, at best, easy-paced.

Playing the same hand in the same way every time has worked.

Swann is the first England spinner to take 25 wickets in an Ashes series since Jim Laker took 46 in 1956; and far more important than the statistics, Swann won the crucial moments for England, by dismissing batsmen whether they had just come in or become well-set.

On the last day at Riverside, when Australia reached 147 for two in pursuit of 311, it was Swann who kept England in the game with those two wickets, until England's seamers – especially Stuart Broad – were stirred to play their part. If they had not been stirred, surely Swann would still have had the final say.

But a five-Test series should be played on five different stages in order to maximise the drama and public interest. Then a series is a true test of the players because it spans a wide range of conditions.

Playing every match on the same sort of pitch – as if England had carted one drop-in pitch to every venue – has resulted in a Pyrrhic victory.

In these circumstances, where the ball has never come on to the bat, England have batted more productively than Australia but not more entertainingly: the tourists have scored well above three runs an over, sometimes collapsing in the process of course, while England have scored well below three.

If a cricket crowd likes nothing better than the sight of a batsman 'on the go', they will remember Michael Clarke at Old Trafford – for Kevin Pietersen's century was an act of self-discipline – or Shane Watson at the Oval, or Ashton Agar's 98, the world Test record for a number 11.

And England's dependence on Swann to do the business on a dry pitch in every match was an admission that Australia's pace bowlers were just as good or better. In itself this admission does not bode well for England's prospects on livelier pitches this winter, given that Swann last time held sway only in Adelaide and had an overall record of 15 wickets at 39.

Whereas Swann fulfilled all the expectations of him, Ian Bell exceeded them and became the man of this series for some great batting. Like no other batsman on either side, he found a way to score consistently on these dry and ever more tiresome pitches.

As a traditional batsman, not a modern bludgeoner, Bell came into this series equipped with two advantages: endless patience, at least until he had reached his century (he has not gone beyond 113), and a late-cut, with which he has scored more than a quarter of his runs to third man.

If this sounds too critical of England's strategy, their way of exploiting home advantage has been usually – if not ever – thus. Defensive batting through the series, then a minefield for their finger-spinners, usually at the Oval: this has been the successful formula in 1926, 1953, 1956, 2009 and 2013.

The glorious uncertainty of cricket is reduced by dry, slow pitches. This is exactly why they were ordered: to eliminate the possibility of Australia winning with their seamers. It is a certainty, however, that England will not have the same pitches prepared next summer for the five-Test series against India, who have Ravi Ashwin and Ravi Jadeja, a fine off-spinner and slow left-armer. Pitches next year will no doubt be as green as this summer's have been brown.

If this series has touched new heights in one particular area, it has been in chasing the ball to the boundary. David

Warner for Australia and Jonny Bairstow for England have raised the bar with their sprinting, headfirst diving, clawing the ball back, then firing it to the keeper. Sport has never seen this combination of skills.

This series has also been notable for DRS taking up too much time; and for the field of play being turned into a school playground or street market when there is a review, or at the fall of a wicket, or the changing of the ball, when subs in bibs – seemingly by the dozen – run on with drinks and towels. It should not be allowed except at the official drinks break in mid-session. Current practice ruins the sanctity of the field and demeans the occasion.

August 25 Shane Warne

Even though Australia have lost this series 3-0 they are in better shape now than they were at the start of the Ashes. They have more clarity both about what their best XI is and their batting order, and that's due to the good Test cricket they have played in the last three matches.

I don't think they fear England any more. Deep down, at the start of the series, they would have worried about how they were going to play James Anderson or bowl to Alastair Cook, Jonathan Trott and Kevin Pietersen, but they have overcome all those concerns and you can sense they believe they can beat England.

Playing better cricket and getting themselves into winning situations in the last three Tests will hold them in good stead for the return series.

Australia, like any team, are more confident at home. They will not ask for pitches to be prepared to suit their own team – they will get what they are given, which is the way it should be – but what people will notice is there is more grass on the pitches in Australia now than there was when England toured a couple of winters ago.

In the last two seasons in Australia the board have wanted a more even contest between bat and ball. Gone are the days when we had flat pitches and batsmen scoring thousands of runs. Now the bowlers are dominating and the batsmen are struggling to average 40. It is a result of the wickets rather than poor batting techniques.

It is going to be hard work for the top three or four batsmen from both teams against quality bowling attacks.

England have won the Ashes this summer because they been the better team in the bigger moments – especially in the first two Tests. Even though England have won the last three Tests 1-0, if you looked at which side won the most sessions you would have to conclude Australia have dominated. They should have won in Manchester and if that had happened they would have regained that winning feeling and had momentum at Durham. With that winning experience at Old Trafford, I believe they would have closed it out at Durham when they were 147 for one in the second innings chasing 299 to win.

England have not played anywhere near as well as they can but still won 3-0. They will be pretty happy because they know they can improve, but they will also be aware it has been a lot closer than the series scoreline suggests.

The reason England have not played to their best is because Australia have not let them. Australia's bowlers have executed some fantastic plans to Cook, Trott, Prior and Pietersen, who apart from the big hundred at Old Trafford has not had much of an impact.

To Cook, Australia have hardly bowled any balls to his pads or above his waist. They have bowled drive balls all the time and had more patience than him. With Trott they have bowled short balls, peppering him at times with leg slips. Michael Clarke's fields to him have been fantastic.

The senior players such as Cook and Trott will want to improve and it will be interesting to see if Australia keep the same tactics on the fast, bouncy pitches Down Under.

Apart from Ian Bell, who has been fantastic, Australia once again have the better numbers but have lost the big moments, a fact I put down to inexperience.

Australia walk away from this series with that experience. The likes of Steve Smith, Nathan Lyon, Ryan Harris (who's been superb) and Chris Rogers have now experienced the intensity of Ashes cricket. All the Aussie players have improved for that reason. They did not match England's intensity in the first two Tests, but have learned how to put themselves into winning positions.

It is really important Australia continue to do that. After the one-dayers here they go to India for another one-day series before a couple of crucial Sheffield Shield games, when a few spots for the first Test will be nailed down.

Australia have chopped and changed a bit, but by doing so they have stumbled across their best team. It will be hard to move Shane Watson from three for the first Ashes Test in November because it has been so long since an Australian scored a century batting in that position. Looking ahead regarding the Australian team, I think Shaun Marsh, Nathan Coulter-Nile, Josh Hazlewood and Fawad Ahmed will all come into consideration for selection and they will all be on display in the one day series – for me, watch out for Coulter-Nile.

Nathan Lyon has been great in this series, but we know that some of the English players struggle against wrist spin, particularly Ian Bell. I would be seriously looking at Ahmed if he does well in the one-dayers.

Darren Lehmann will have a pretty good idea of his best XI now. With Boof there is no malice in anything he does. He is a knockabout guy who talks straight. We really like that and we have to be careful. If we censor people or jump on top of them for having a bit of banter with the media then they are going to change and you will get the stock, robotic answers. But what Boof also has to remember is he is now the coach of the Australian cricket team and has to be a bit careful in what he says – even if it is in jest.

The Broad incident is just a little tap on the wrist. Have fun and banter, but be a bit careful.

Day Five

August 26 Derek Pringle

Australia (492-9d & 111-6d)
draw with England (377 & 206-5)

Some will argue that cricket was not the winner at the Kia Oval last night, after the final Investec Test was called off for bad light with England needing 21 runs from four overs. But given the home side's intransigence earlier in the match, a draw was the just result.

It was 7.35pm when Aleem Dar took the players off at the Kia Oval to mass booing from the capacity crowd. England were on the brink of their fourth win of the series, a magnitude of victory never achieved previously by them in an Ashes series, and their supporters felt cheated.

But like parasites feeding off a munificent host, Alastair Cook's team have made precious little running in this match and it was only Michael Clarke's declaration which gave them any hope of redemption and the crowd any chance of entertainment.

Clarke would have felt impelled to set up a game following his team's criticism of England's negative tactics with bat and ball earlier in the match, but he did not deserve to get booed for his part. Setting his opponents 228 in a minimum of 44 overs he and his bowlers kept up a rate of 13.04 overs an hour, which was not many below the 15 overs expected, slowing only when it became obvious that light was an issue. But frustrating as it was for England as well as their legions of fans when Dar decided to call it off, once his light meter had dipped below a certain level, umpires cannot bend the laws because history beckons and the home crowd wants their team to win.

International sport cannot be ruled by the mob. It was only eight years ago, in that ding-dong 2005 Ashes series, that England's supporters at the Oval cheered to the rafters when bad light stopped play. But then a draw suited them that day.

The frustration shown by the fans, whose appetite had no doubt been whetted by Kevin Pietersen's brilliant 62 off 55 balls, did not take any gloss off the presentation of the many trophies, including a replica of the famous urn. England have won the series 3-0, a resounding scoreline given Australia had a first-innings lead on four occasions and the home side never once passed 400 in the series. The last time England failed to make 400 in a summer was in 1999, when they were at their lowest ebb of recent times, so this win was as much about prestidigitation as planning.

Their secret has been to win the big moments in the series – the pressure cooker last day at Trent Bridge; the after-tea session on the last day at Durham, to name just two. Your best players tend to clinch those moments and James Anderson, Stuart Broad and Ian Bell grabbed the opportunities well, with Bell deservedly, along with Australia's Ryan Harris, man of the series.

In Ashes series the end justifies the means and this was not a glorious exhibition of cricket like the 2005 series. England were efficient in matches that were not brimming with quality.

England's 'we have what we hold' mentality, and they held the Ashes coming into this series, meant that the pitches were dry, slow turners, suited to Graeme Swann and not many others. Unsurprisingly Swann had his best ever series with 26 wickets, a superb effort following the operation to his right elbow just three months previously.

After retaining the Ashes at Old Trafford and winning the series at Durham, this Test was meant to provide a crowning moment for England, though one that quickly dissipated after Australia had made 492 in the first innings.

It is not often that parts of the last three innings occur on the final day of a Test, but after Friday's go-slow by England, Saturday's washout, and Australia's desire to finish the series with a flicker of fire, these were exceptional circumstances.

Australia had to get England out first once play had got under way at 11.30am, following a period of mopping up the heavy overnight rain. If the groundstaff at the Kia Oval did a good job, so did Ian Bell in seeing his team past the follow-on target of 292. Once that had been achieved, the onus was on Australia, a realisation that enabled England's batsmen to bat more freely than at any other time in the match, the last four batsman adding 78 runs in 16 overs. Their first innings closed on 377, a deficit of 115.

With a day's play missed, the pitch was not as worn as usual, so Clarke had to leave England a target they might be tempted by to get wickets rather than to rely on the ball misbehaving. Before four-day cricket, county captains were expert in judging what to leave their opponents, something Clarke seemed unsure of despite promoting his biffers up the order.

Clarke declared during the tea interval, setting England 227 to win in a minimum of 44 overs. Cook and Joe Root gave England a solid start while Australia attacked in the hunt for wickets, though Root went in the 50th over flapping at Harris to give Brad Haddin his 29th catch of the series and beat Rod Marsh's Ashes record of 28 set in the 1982-83 series.

Cook and Trott then elevated the platform with a stand of 64 in 15 overs before Cook was lbw playing all round one from Faulkner. Then the pyrotechnics began with Pietersen's fizzing Catherine wheel offset by Jonathan Trott's steady candle before Bell's sparkler promised to write four-nil into the darkening sky. But just as a ground-breaking victory beckoned, the light, despite the use of floodlights, became too bad for the red ball and the game was abandoned as a draw.

August 26 Paul Hayward

Ask the cricket public to describe this England team and the answers are 'efficient' and 'functional' as well as 'winners' and 'better than Australia'.

There is accuracy but not much warmth in those responses. Until this classic Oval drama Alastair Cook's men were struggling to 'urn' the nation's love. Folk hero status has been denied this England side, despite the grandeur of their record. Here in Kennington, scene of many a last-day thriller, they endeavoured to join the 2005 and 2009 teams in the scrapbook of happy English summers before bad light brought an agonising end to their quest.

Somehow Australia managed to turn a 115-run lead into a desperate survival exercise, despite batting a second time in between. Arch opportunists that they are, England accepted the challenge of chasing 227 in 45 overs. Just when people have labelled them cautious miserabilists, out they come with blades flashing. Kevin Pietersen's 62 off 55 balls was a masterclass in precise machismo.

And yet there is a curious disconnect between this team and their public which Cook's men would do well to correct on the winter's tour to Australia. Pietersen's batting here in 2005 and Stuart Broad's bowling four years later were the rallying points in what felt like national rebirths. Now, for the most part, England go about the business of maintaining their superiority over Australia like a crack team of engineers.

To the outside eye they are a closed society, as poor Simon Kerrigan probably discovered. They move about in hedgehog formation. They have their own codes and are suspicious of outsiders. The public can count their runs and wickets but know little of their characters. Press conferences tend to yield only platitudes and interviews often come with heavy sponsor messages attached. The Australian cricket writer Malcolm Conn wrote that under questioning England were as 'colourful as a concrete driveway'. In other words they are strong in character, comfortable in their own skin in their own sealed-off world and highly adept at strategy. Managing the ball, devising ways to remove batsmen and making sure that someone always plays well enough to make up for the failures of others in the side are all now second nature. Australia have been sent home without a Test win for the first time since 1977. Such feats are not to be obscured by grumbles about how joyless they sometimes are.

This final gave us a taste of how it could be. More joie de vivre and less calculation were on display. The punters who stuck with English cricket though the barren years should not have to put with a team being negative, prickly and remote.

Earlier in this series Shane Warne wrote on these pages: 'A lot of us reporting and commentating on the game were really taken aback by the way the England players were interviewing and behaving in press conferences and after-match interviews.

'Yes, England are a very good cricket team and it is their choice how they convey messages to the press and act on and off the field, and also how they want to represent themselves individually and collectively as a team. But to me there were a few moments at Old Trafford when I thought, "Hang on, who do you think you are?"'

Plainly some feel under-appreciated. They ask how a winning side can be upbraided. They fail to see how the dips in form by Alastair Cook, Jonathan Trott or Matt Prior can be an issue when Australia have not won a Test. But they also seem incapable of understanding why the Oval crowd might bridle at being told England would be going all out for the 4-0 win, only to see them score 215 in a 98-over day, after their bowlers strangled the over rate on Thursday.

'Any time they get threatened they go into their shell and play defensive cricket,' argued Australia's James Faulkner, who is pretty chirpy for a debutante. 'When they come to Australia it will be played on our terms. They will be in for a hell of a challenge.' England will chuckle at that. The Australian collapse at Lord's seemed to plant in English heads the idea that they could not lose to such a rabble.

'Not as good as they think they are,' is another popular verdict on Cook's team. But they are also as good as they need to be; and, often, no more than that. They play in spurts, winning the decisive phases, with no heed of any obligation to entertain.

Nothing wrong with that, generally, except that they will never find out how good they are if they keep the shutters down. Stuart Broad, who performs the ant-hero's role with great aplomb, was scuffling with critical spectators on twitter on Friday night, telling one: 'You're obviously not a true England fan. We do have a win-at-all-costs mentality. We want to win, we want to make the fans happy,' Broad said.

The first part may be true but there is little evidence that the second occupies their thoughts much. The personality of their coach, Andy Flower, is apparent in the leaning towards efficiency. But if there is one phrase to describe what they might do in Australia, to show themselves to their disciples, it is: Lighten up.

August 26 Scyld Berry

Test cricket is at its best when the players of both sides have been placed in a situation which neither they nor any previous cricketers have ever known before.

It was the 2094th Test, and never before had the equation been 227 off 44 overs. It was fairly similar at Centurion in

2000 but then Hansie Cronje, South Africa's captain, was fixed on not drawing the game.

So at the Oval theatre, the last act of this series had no script. The coaches could not tell their players anything of specific relevance from their experience. The players could not be programmed.

And such uncertainty on a late August evening, born of Michael Clarke's daring declaration, riveted all concerned. At the end of an over when the PA announcer tried to tell the crowd about the ceremonies that would take place at the finish, such was the clapping, cheering and chanting that not one of his words was audible.

It was drama – and, better still, the drama of the first-night play, when none of the audience knows the outcome. Or rather, best of all, a play in which nobody – neither the audience nor the actors – knows what the outcome will be.

Kevin Pietersen did his best to script the finish. When he came in, England wanted 141 runs from the last 145 balls of the series, although there was always the likelihood that fading light would shave off a few overs.

Cometh the hour, cometh the showman. Pietersen feels good at the Oval: not only his breakthrough innings of 158 in 2005, but his first Test here as captain when he made a century against South Africa, and won. He not only averages more than 60 runs per innings here but, thanks to some pace in the pitch, four runs per over.

During his 55 balls, Pietersen could hardly have done more to recreate the magic of his innings eight years ago.

But there was one difference between then and now. This Australian side have not been able to bat like their predecessors, or bowl Shane Warne, but their ground-fielding has been superlative.

In 2005 Pietersen was dropped more than once when the match was far from safe. On Sunday evening the first time he hit the ball towards a fielder, he was caught by David Warner at long-on.

Jonathan Trott had contributed 13 to their partnership of 77 and, being mortal, could not accelerate as his partner had. The next two Warwickshire players, Ian Bell and Chris Woakes, stayed on course to knock off the runs in 44 overs, but not in the 40 overs that approaching autumn allowed, before the script decreed the curtain should come down.

Before Pietersen, England's captain Alastair Cook had found some fluency for the first time in this series. Even though he did not 'go on', once again, Cook did enough – in addition to his conscientious captaincy – to merit being one of the opening batsman in a composite eleven made up of these two sides.

Chris Rogers, though demoted on Sunday, would be Cook's partner. Shane Watson was man of this match for his 176, and he can bowl better than Trott. Watson's spell last evening was wicketless, as usual, yet invaluable.

Pietersen's conversation with Michael Clarke, when they partner each other at four and five, would be worth turning up the stump-mike for. And when one of them runs the other out, there is always Bell to make another hundred.

Brad Haddin's record feat, of making the most dismissals

in any Test series, was overlooked in the closing ceremonies: no wonder wicketkeepers are used to being neglected. Haddin made his 29 catches off nine different bowlers, but most of them – nine – off Ryan Harris.

Harris, the bustling bull-dog with no bite, took 24 wickets in only four Tests. He and James Anderson would be a pace attack to avoid, backed by Stuart Broad who improved as the series went on, whereas Peter Siddle faded.

And who else but Graeme Swann, the leading wicket-taker with 26, to be the spinner? Didn't he love being in control?

Composite XI: Cook, Rogers, Watson, Pietersen, Clarke (capt), Bell, Haddin, Broad, Swann, Harris and Anderson.

August 26 Geoffrey Boycott

Well done England for not playing your best but still winning 3-0. A lot of people are talking about Australia going home with some plusses and how they will be better equipped to compete with us at home this winter.

But hang on a minute. We can play a lot better, too. We have experienced, big scoring batsmen in Alastair Cook, Jonathan Trott and Matt Prior who have played way below their normal standards.

If we can pick ourselves up and get our best batsmen playing to their ability it does not matter how much improvement Australia make, we will still be good enough to beat them providing we do not make any more selection blunders.

It has not been a memorable series. The expectation has outweighed the reality. What we have seen are moments of drama, sweet batting from Ian Bell, quality bowling by James Anderson, Stuart Broad and Graeme Swann and in between times some fairly average cricket.

Australia's batting was as poor as I expected it to be and all the hype about the new coach Darren Lehmann, who people like and admire, has proved again that he cannot bat and bowl for his team. It all comes down to the 11 on the field. They can spout off about how they are going to undermine Broad, and get the crowd behind them in Australia but it will not make any difference unless their players outplay ours.

England are battle hardened and the only thing they have to do is do what they have done in this series, play better than Australia.

Australia can talk all they want. They have to deliver it on the field and they have not done that against England for a many years.

Continuity has been an England trait under Andy Flower. They have always liked a four-man attack, and once you got in the team, it was hard to get out of it.

With a 3-0 lead in the bag they did a lot of talking before the final Test about being positive and wanting to win this last match. As soon as they saw a dry pitch they thought 'play two spinners'. Monty Panesar has problems and could not play. He would have been ideal here. Instead Simon Kerrigan was selected and England wanted to be brave and go for a win. All very nice but then someone must have said 'just a minute, we will only have five batsmen and three of them are out of nick.'

Suddenly caution took over England's thinking. Then they said 'let's have a safety valve.' A guy who can bat as well as bowl so Chris Woakes got in the team. It did not matter that he cannot bowl anyone out at international level. England decided 'we don't want to be beaten by this lot.' Once England lost the toss their chance of winning the Test disappeared. Why? Because after one hour of superb seam bowling with the new ball by Anderson and Broad that unluckily only brought one wicket, we did not have an attacking wicket-taking seam bowler to keep the pressure on Australia's batsmen.

Woakes is a good all-round cricketer. He is an English-type seamer who would have bowled very well years ago when Tests started with pitches a bit damp, grassier and certainly when we played on uncovered pitches open to the rain.

Nowadays surfaces have better preparation, they have marvellous covering when it is raining and are so dry that matches could start at 10am. Channelling money to all the Test grounds to improve the outfield drainage is one of the best things the ECB has done in recent years.

The days of seaming pitches have gone. Now you need some pace, allied to natural movement. Modest medium pace like Woakes will not cut it. He is a batsman and an occasional fourth seamer for international cricket. He will not be a big wicket taker at this level.

Kerrigan's bowling was a nightmare. It was embarrassing to watch. We can all sympathise with his stage fright and nerves. To watch that young man have the worst cricketing experience of his life was not pleasant. But it was not all his fault. Our selectors have to accept a great deal of responsibility and criticism for putting him in that situation.

The real skill in being a selector is not just to look at how many wickets a bowler has taken and his average. What you need to do is analyse his action, check on his character and mental toughness and then make a judgement as to whether that player is equipped to make the step up from second division championship cricket to Test cricket. England's selectors failed that test badly.

We have not had a blunder as bad as this since someone had the bright idea to pick an unknown bowler called Darren Pattinson for a Test match at Headingley against South Africa in 2008. He was picked because he could swing the ball. He did swing it all right. Smack bang into the middle of the South African bats.

A big positive for me at the Oval was seeing Joe Root make a really big effort to get his feet apart, particularly playing forward. It was obvious he was making a conscious effort and if he keeps working on that he will only get better. It is not going to come overnight and it is a work in progress.